TOOLS FOR
CONFLICT RESOLUTION

A Prased on
Phe

Published in the United States of America
by ScarecrowEducation
An imprint of The Rowman & Littlefield Publishing Group, Inc.
4501 Forbes Boulevard, Suite 200, Lanham, Maryland 20706
www.scarecroweducation.com

PO Box 317
Oxford
OX2 9RU, UK

British Library Cataloguing in Publication Information Available

Library of Congress Cataloging-in-Publication Data

O'Keefe, Ellen M., 1954–
  Tools for conflict resolution : a practical K–12 program based on
Peter Senge's 5th discipline / Ellen M. O'Keefe, Mary Catherine Stewart.
    p. cm.
  Includes bibliographical references and index.
  ISBN 1-57886-110-1 (paperback : alk. paper)
  1. Classroom environment. 2. Conflict management—Study and teaching.
3. Lesson planning. I. Stewart, Mary Catherine, 1952– II. Senge, Peter M.
Fifth discipline. III. Title.
LB3013 .O34 2004
371.3'028—dc22

                                                            2003024144

CONTENTS

ACKNOWLEDGMENTS

We wish to thank the Springfield Dominican Community, which introduced Sr. Mary Catherine to Peter Senge's mental models and the ladder of inference. She was so energized by the material that she came to believe that if students, parents, and teachers could learn to use the tools, our world would be a much happier place.

We would also like to thank the Education Division at Mount Mercy College. The enthusiasm they showed from the day we first offered to write the book until the day of the book's completion has helped us to continue our work. They listened to us worry about the formatting, plans, and deadlines. They helped us with ideas for literature and activities when we asked them. It has been comforting to have this support from our colleagues.

Next, we would like to thank the education students at Mount Mercy College, who learned to use the mental model tools and shared their heartwarming, humorous stories with us as they tried to use the mental model tools.

Mark Benesh is a student at Mount Mercy College who, although he has a family, agreed to illustrate our book. His creative characters that enhanced our ideas continuously impressed us.

We would like to acknowledge the professionals at ScarecrowEducation, in particular, Cindy Tursman, for her work with us. She answered

any questions we had and encouraged us in every way possible. Her attention and caring were encouragement in itself.

We owe a huge thanks to each other: Ellen O'Keefe, who was willing
to "adventure" with me as we prepared a proposal for an Association of
Supervision and Curriculum Development conference, presented our
ideas at the conference, and did the detail work that made this book possible; Sr. Catherine for her creativity, enthusiasm, and for being such a
positive person to work with in cowriting this book.

Of course, we would be remiss if we didn't thank family and friends,
who consistently asked, "How is the book coming along?" Many times,
as we observed interactions between close friends and family, new ideas
for the book were generated. We are grateful to the many people who
have shared their conflict stories with us over the years.

Finally, we would like to thank our mothers. They have listened to us
talk about the process of writing this book as well as the content of this
book, and they have offered positive feedback and attitudes. Our mothers have always provided us with unconditional love and support for any
endeavor we pursued.

1

AN INTRODUCTION TO MENTAL MODELS AND THE DEVELOPMENTAL APPROPRIATENESS OF THEIR APPLICATION

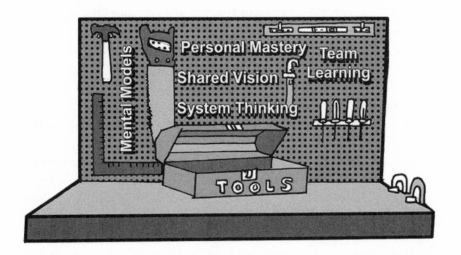

Throughout our entire educational careers, we spent many moments assisting a variety of people in solving conflicts. We worked with students and heard the age-old cry "It's not my fault, she/he hit me first." Parents often came into our classrooms and discussed the conflicts between themselves and their spouses or between themselves and their children. Faculty room discussion often centered on conflicts between staff members, between administration and faculty, or between faculty and students. Conflict stories were found in abundance. However, solutions and programs to assist both young and old in developing conflict resolution skills were scarce.

One day, we picked up *Schools That Learn* by Peter Senge. We were very excited; in this book was a theory that held many possibilities for teaching conflict resolution skills. We began to envision a creative, practical program that allows students and adults to develop life-long conflict resolution skills using the "five disciplines."

This chapter introduces the five disciplines and gives a basic theoretical framework on which the program is built. It is probably the least practical of all of the chapters, but it is necessary for understanding the five disciplines as tools for developing conflict management skills. If we can help students focus on and practice specific conflict management skills at school, hopefully, the skills will become automatic and students will naturally use this type of thinking in their workplaces and homes as adults.

The first discipline that becomes our first tool is personal mastery. Personal mastery is the practice of keeping one's dreams alive while being grounded in our daily routines. As adults and students work toward achieving their dreams, the ordinary daily events become stepping-stones toward the dream. No longer is there a dichotomy between reality and the dream; rather the two concepts are blended into a transformative process. For example, many teachers at the beginning of the school year are asked to write a professional development plan for the year and hand it in to their principal. After reflecting on his/her strengths and weaknesses, the teacher may write: (1) I will incorporate cooperative learning groups into my teaching this year, and (2) I will teach my students how to do peer evaluation on writing samples using a rubric. The key to personal mastery is self-reflection. In our instant world, it is imperative for teachers to give students time to reflect on who they are (present strengths and weaknesses) and who they are becoming (practical ways to enrich strengths and improve weaknesses).

Our second tool is mental models, which also happens to be the second discipline. Mental models are usually stored in our unconscious. People are unaware of operating out of them until someone brings the mental models to their attention. Mental models are composed of values, beliefs, assumptions, and attitudes. It is because of mental models that two people can observe the same event and describe it differently. In essence, our mental models are like lenses. We make sense out of new experiences by pulling the new information through our existing mental models. The new information solidifies a preexisting mental model.

Many of our stereotypical beliefs grow out of this concept. In a classroom, there is a child who always comes to school very dirty and unkempt. We know from previous years of teaching that this child will fail. All children who come from lower socioeconomic homes have a difficult time in school. We are sure this child will fall into that pattern.

The positive attributes of mental models are: (1) they give us "hooks" on which to hang new information, (2) they allow us to categorize new information quickly, and (3) they help us feel comfortable in new situations. The largest negative attribute of mental models is they help us resist change. We become so comfortable with the lens we use that we don't want to use a different lens. Most of the time, the assumptions and judgments we make are made so quickly that we are unaware of the mental model construct we are using.

To examine our mental models, we must be willing to engage in a two-step process. The first step of the process is to become a reflective practitioner. Whenever we are making assumptions or judgments, we need to ask ourselves how we just formed that particular idea. What experience, value, or belief led us to that conclusion? The second step of the process is to engage in inquiry. The inquiry must be done in a nonthreatening, safe environment. In this stage, people need to feel free to ask each other, "What experience, value, or belief led you to that conclusion?" Neither of these steps come automatically. Everyone must agree that she/he wants to engage in the process. Once everyone decides to participate in the process, becoming aware of mental model constructs and recognizing the patterns become almost second nature for those involved. The results are fewer assumptions and judgments and increased open communication skills.

The mental model that is used most frequently is the "ladder of inference." According to this model, most of our decisions, assumptions, and judgments are based on four premises:

- Our beliefs are *the* truth.
- The truth is obvious.
- Our beliefs are based on real data.
- The data we select are the real data. (Senge et al., 2000, p. 68)

As an example, consider a student whose father died. This student had a difficult time handling his grief. During this time, he frequently missed class. One day, he showed up for class; we were doing small group work. In the middle of class, he gathered his books together and left. As he left, I asked, "Ben, what's wrong?" He replied: "I'm just so tired." Ben did not return to class the next three class periods. During this time, I called his home and left messages for him to call back. He did not return the calls. I thought that he had "written me off" and wanted to isolate himself. During this entire situation, I climbed up the "ladder of inference."

- My observable data was: Ben walked out in the middle of my class.
- The details I selected about Ben's behavior were his response, "I'm just so tired," and Ben's refusal to return my calls. (I didn't know his answering machine was not working correctly and he didn't receive any of my messages.)
- Based upon my college culture, I added these meanings: polite students always return calls. Ben is writing me off and wants to isolate himself.
- I decided that Ben didn't want me to contact him and hates me.

By the time I reached the top of the ladder, I was angry with Ben and had decided to write *him* off—"he can fail my course." In looking at this scenario, it is easy to see that, in a case such as this, most of the climb up the ladder is accomplished through an internal process. No one on the outside can see the details I've selected or the meanings I've added. Rarely do I stop to reflect on the validity of this internal process. The only external features in this model are the observable data and the action I take after I climb the ladder.

Day after day, month after month, and year after year, most of us climb the ladder of inference without being aware of how it affects our relationships with others. Once we become aware of the tool, we are able to stop ourselves and reexamine the data we've selected, the meanings we've added, and the conclusions we've drawn. Those processes are a normal part of everyday life. What we can do is question ourselves and others about the data we've selected, the meanings we've added, and the conclusions we've drawn. Let's return to the Ben scenario for a moment. I reexamined the conclusion and decided that there might be a different reason for Ben's unresponsiveness. I sent a note to Ben and asked him to please contact me. I explained that I had called him several times and that I needed to know how he was going to handle his missing assignments. Ben contacted me at home and thanked me for persevering in trying to contact him. He explained that his answering machine was not working. He had not received any of my phone calls. If I had not been exposed to the notion of the ladder of inference and had not taken a few moments to reexamine my conclusions, I would have continued to carry a negative attitude toward Ben.

If an entire faculty or classroom of students agrees to learn the ladder of inference, each person can assist the other person in recognizing "ladder patterns" by asking a few simple questions. The questions might be similar to these: (1) What are the observable data? (2) Is everyone willing to agree that what is listed are the observable data? (3) Can you model your thinking process so we can understand the meanings you've added? There may not be time for all of the questions, so another option is to test the meanings you've added to the observable data by using an open-ended question. Once again, let's look at the Ben scenario. If I had accidentally run into Ben, I might have said to him "Ben, you're not returning any of my calls. Are you "writing me off?"

Once we begin to become comfortable with "thinking aloud," it is easier to see both the differences and the commonalities of our perceptions. It's easier to discuss issues we feel strongly about and negotiate compromise once we understand the variety of perceptions that surround a single issue.

Some people find it a little intimidating to begin practicing ladder of inference skills. There is another tool that can ease people into learning the ladder of inference. That tool is known as the left-hand/right-hand column. In this process, one simply writes a conversation as it occurred in the right-hand column. After it is written, a person goes back and writes feelings and thoughts that weren't expressed in the left-hand column. Let's look at an example (see table 1.1).

Table 1.1. The Left-Hand/Right-Hand Column

Left-Hand Column	Right-Hand Column
What I'm thinking	What is said
I'm embarrassed that I was tagged out, so I'll blame Chris.	Ben: Geez, Chris. Why did you get in my way?
Chris always gets his way—he's bigger than me but I'll show him that I'm bigger—I'll intimidate him!	Chris: It's not my fault—you're always in the way—you big oaf!
	Ben: If you knew what was good for you, you'd leave NOW!
Great, now I'm really embarrassed. I'm the one looking like the bad guy.	Chris: (walking away) Ben, you are the biggest baby I have ever met!

For some people, it's easier to begin with this process, because it is written rather than oral. Introverts need time to reflect before speaking. This tool allows a person to move through the process at his/her own speed. Once a person becomes comfortable with this process, she/he finds it easier to move into sharing this process with another and, finally, to move into the ladder of inference, which is an oral process. However, extroverts will probably find it easier to use the ladder of inference. Both processes are equally valuable. Neither is better than the other. Both attempt to model thinking processes that shape and mold our perceptions.

So far in our toolbox, we have personal mastery, the ladder of inference, and the right-hand/left-hand column. The next tool we shall examine is "shared vision." Shared vision is a group of people working together to create an "end dream" and deciding on the necessary steps along the way for achieving the end dream. In a classroom, the students and teachers together might decide that the end dream is to respect all people and materials.

On the first day of school, the teacher and students sit down and discuss how they want to achieve this goal this year. Together, the students and the teacher create rules and consequences that assist everyone in attaining this dream.

Shared vision often flows out of another discipline: "team building." Sit back and reflect for a moment. Our schools are filled with teams: teachers often design lessons for cooperative learning teams; teachers often plan together in teams; principals from different buildings often work as an administrative team; and a large team consisting of the superintendent and the school board runs the entire school district. Considering the number of teams everyone experiences, one might conclude that this tool is easy to use and that team skills are developed automatically without any practice. Nothing could be further from the truth. Team learning is dependent upon conversational skills. Inherent to conversational skills is the practice of dialogue. "The goal of dialogue is to open new ground by establishing a 'container' or 'field' for inquiry; a setting where people can become more aware of the context around their experience, and of the processes of thought and feeling that created that experience" (W. Isaacs, cited in Senge et al. 2000, 75). Before dialogue can really happen, those participating must feel safe. Creating a safe environment is necessary before beginning to use any of the tools. One way to do this is to establish a daily "check-in." Students and teacher(s) form a circle. Each person shares whatever she/he chooses. If a person chooses not to share, she/he simply says, "pass." A check-in simply allows people a few moments to focus on what is important at this point in time. Once everyone is comfortable sharing, it is easy to move to the next step of sharing assumptions. Dialogue carries the ladder of inference one step further and gives each person the opportunity to bring assumptions to the surface, to name the assumptions, and finally, to have others assist one in stretching and changing his/her assumptions by engaging in inquiry regarding the assumptions. In most dialogues, members can hear when each person is speaking from the heart and can understand each person's position and how she/he arrived at it, once assumptions are shared.

Another set of skills that help establish a true dialogue are inquiry and advocacy skills. The characterization of these skills is very simple: "Here is my view and here is how I have arrived at it. How does it sound to you? What makes sense to you and what doesn't? Do you see any ways I can improve it?" (Senge et al. 2000, 219). There are a myriad of practical phrases that can be used to develop this process that will be covered in a separate chapter.

Our final tool is "systems thinking." Systems have been around for a long time. We are surrounded by a variety of systems—ecological, family, school, and so forth. Systems thinking is "the ability to understand (and sometimes to predict) interactions and relationships in complex, dynamic systems: the kinds of systems we are surrounded by and embedded in" (Senge et al. 2000, 239). In looking at systems thinking, we are going to examine two processes that assist people in understanding relationships. Behavior over time graphs help in understanding the patterns of change over time as well as what is happening in the system; causal-loop diagrams show ways that "different elements in a system influence one another" (Senge et al. 2000, 242). Causal loops actually tell us "why" a particular action is occurring.

In conclusion, our toolbox is filled with five very important tools for solving conflicts. These tools are: (1) personal mastery; (2) mental models, which includes the processes of the ladder of inference and right-hand–left-hand column; (3) shared vision; (4) team building, which includes dialogue as well as advocacy and inquiry processes; and (5) systems thinking, which includes the behavior over time graphs and causal-loop diagrams.

Let's examine each tool with a developmentally appropriate lens. At what age or what grade level should children be given these tools? At what stage will children begin to develop some of these tools, and how can we as educators provide experiences that strengthen this development?

The first developmental stage we shall examine is from birth to approximately age four. During this stage, a child's cognitive process develops in three distinct ways. The child begins to make comparisons: my mother's face has a nose, my father's face has a nose, and my face has a nose or my mother has fingers, my father has fingers, I have fingers. Slowly, the child begins to be aware of the interrelationships in his/her world. At this stage, the child is most concerned about him/herself.

Babies often play with blocks, stacking them from largest to smallest. Through this activity, they are beginning to learn sequential thinking. Sequential thinking will continue to develop throughout the child's life, but particularly in the primary years. At the age of four, the child begins to understand stories and notice a simple sequence of events. It's important for parents, when reading to a child, to ask, "What happened first?" and "What happened next?" As a parent dresses a child in the morning, she/he might ask, "What do I put on you first?" "What's the last thing I put on you?"

During this time, the child is very egocentric. She/he connects everything she/he sees, experiences, or does to how she/he feels. The child naturally progresses through these stages; however, it is very important for the teacher or parent to spend time with the child, asking simple questions so the child continues to develop.

At this age, children also develop mental models about the world that surrounds them. Aunt Bessie left the room; that must mean she is unhappy. As children grow, they begin to distinguish between when Aunt Bessie left the room because she was upset and when she left because she had a job to do in a different part of the house.

At this age level, children need structure and rules. At this developmental stage, parents and teachers do not incorporate a shared vision process. For the most part, teachers and parents tell children what they will do. Around the age of four, parents and teachers need to explain to children why they are telling them to do a certain action. Children are developing the ability to understand the reason behind the action and this helps them as they become capable of participating in a shared vision process.

Let's look at the next stage, grades K–2, or ages five to seven. Sequential thinking continues to grow and develop. It's very important at this stage for teachers and parents to provide numerous activities for the child to continue to develop this skill.

During these years, children remain egocentric. They begin to develop awareness that there are other people around them and that there are other students in other grades; however, there is not an interest in those children.

At this stage, parents and teachers need to become reflective coaches. After a child finishes an activity, either parent or teacher needs to ask "What was the easiest part for you?" or "What was the hardest part for you?" or "How do you feel now that it's finished?" The ladder of inference is a reflective tool—"What did you actually see that anyone would have seen?" (Senge et al. 2000, 157). Adults need to help children begin to think about their own thinking. It's very important for children to realize that how they process information is often more important than the end result.

Students can also be introduced to systems thinking. Children are aware of patterns. By creating visual patterns, children begin to see the interrelationships between causes and effects. For example, first graders can map different types of animals and the kinds of food they eat. Then they can group and map the types of habitats where the different animals are found, based on the location of their food.

As the child continues to grow, we find him/her beginning to collect things—rocks, McDonald's Happy Meal gifts, trains, dolls, toys of all shapes and sizes. At this point, the child is moving into the intermediate developmental stage, and she/he will be in grades 3–5 and between the ages of eight and eleven. Collecting is a need that is actually driving him/her into the verbal reasoning stage. The child is beginning to move from the concrete stage of thinking into the abstract stage of thinking. She/he is developing the ability to think about five or more things at one time and is beginning to make connections between the ideas or concepts. At this stage, the more time that a child spends classifying different ideas or items in different ways, the faster she/he will move into the next stage.

Verbal reasoning skills continue to develop from this point onward. These verbal reasoning skills do not develop automatically. Parents and teachers need to provide experiences that help the child develop these skills. Parents and teachers need to engage children in dialogue. Asking a child to "tell me a story" is just one of many ways to develop these skills. Children who have received guidance and coaching at the previous levels have a solid foundation on which to build these new skills. Parents and teachers need to remain reflective coaches throughout the child's entire growth and developmental process.

As one would expect, the child's emotional awareness continues to develop. There is an interesting phenomenon in which a child, as she/he begins to move out of the egocentric stage, more often than not will try to cling to that stage. Family traditions become very important. For example, we celebrate Christmas the same way each year. The way that we do it defines who we are. If we change it, then we won't be the same family.

As the child becomes aware that there are many different perspectives, she/he will try to hold onto the "one way" of looking at life. At the same time, the child begins to appreciate the differences she/he notices. The child begins to ask his/her friends "Why do two people have different ideas even though they watched the same movie?" or "Why do we feel more comfortable in Teacher A's class than Teacher B's class?"

Beginning in third grade, the child becomes aware of the difference between his/her imagination and reality. Santa Claus, the Tooth Fairy, and the Easter Bunny are imaginary characters and are no longer "real." The child realizes that she/he can enter an imaginary world through a movie or a television show and then reenter the real world after the show is over.

As we mentioned earlier, teachers and parents need to continue the reflective coaching at this stage. Parents and teachers may accomplish this not only by asking questions, but also by sharing observations that will help children understand themselves better. Let's say your child has a group of friends over for the evening. You notice your child spends more time with Joe and Mike and little or no time with John. However, Joe and Mike seem to include John in everything. After the boys leave, you casually mention to your son what you noticed. You make no comment as to "right" or "wrong" and you ask no probing questions; you just give your son the opportunity to reflect on your observation.

The ladder of inference becomes a very important tool. However, children can easily justify all of their thoughts, so don't assume that getting the children to climb down the ladder is going to be easy. But with practice and continual coaching, the ladder of inference is a very effective tool that can be used by the entire family.

In the case of personal mastery, the key word at this stage is "choose." Teachers and parents need to structure choices so that, no matter how a child chooses, she/he is going to grow. Not only is it important for the child to make the choice, but also it's crucial for the parent or teacher to spend time with the child reflecting on the choice she/he made.

- What were you trying to accomplish? What were you hoping would happen? (vision)
- What actually happened? Were you disappointed? If so, why? What's changed? How do you think about that change? (current reality)
- Could your expectations have been different? How might you have set it up differently? What do you want to try next? (priorities) (Senge et al. 2000, 161)

As far as cooperative learning is concerned, kindergarten, first-grade, and second-grade students enjoy working in groups; however, they will divide the work and each do a part. Beginning in third grade, students begin to recognize and affirm each other's gifts. Students know who writes well, who illustrates well, who sees the whole project and knows how to put it together, and who organizes well. Students working in groups no longer divide up the work, but work together capitalizing on each other's strengths. This process continues to develop, and by fourth and fifth grade, students are ready and able to work on open-ended projects. Teachers can tell students what the expected end is and allow students to develop the process to achieve the end. Students are able to discuss ideas as equals; no longer is one student "the boss," telling everyone what to do.

Beginning in third grade, students are able to create, with their teacher, classroom rules and consequences. Students know the type of environment in which they wish to learn. By creating the classroom environment together, students have a greater sense of belonging that in turn creates a greater sense of trust and respect.

Third grade is also the age in which students enjoy graphic organizers. Mapping, scaffolding, webbing, outlining, and similar activities help students make visual connections. The students are already engaged in creating internal connections, and the graphic organizers are one way to share those connections with others. Systems thinking is built upon this foundation. Together, graphic organizers and systems thinking language help students articulate their newly developing reasoning skills.

Along comes adolescence, and with it comes a myriad of changes. Students are no longer comfortable in their own skins. Physically, they are trying out all sorts of products to make them "perfect teens." Their thought processes are becoming more abstract, and they are beginning to see how much there is in the world to learn. Up until this time, students for the most part have been in self-contained classrooms. Now they are moving from teacher to teacher, and with that movement comes the need to develop relational skills. Not only do students need to adjust to each teacher's personality and educational expectations, but they must also develop the skills to relate with a cross-section of their peers. Students must continue to make choices based on their values, beliefs, hopes, and dreams, but they must also learn how to discuss these concepts in a diverse environment. How do I talk about and accept values that are different from the ones I hold? How do I validate another's dreams even though I know I would never personally follow that dream?

As students move into this new stage of development, parents and teachers must move from a facilitating and monitoring role to a mentoring role. With time and practice, everyone can make this transition. Teachers and parents can no longer dictate to students as they did in the past. It is important to create common goals with students and to be accessible in helping them achieve these goals. Keeping the lines of communication open is important during this stage of development.

During the junior high and high school years, students are very engaged in personal mastery. Students are looking at possible careers and are trying to decide if they have the gifts necessary to attend the college of their choice and receive a degree that will allow them to work in the career of their dreams. Parents and teachers need to provide experiences that help students realistically reflect on their personal strengths and weaknesses and articulate their personal dreams.

Mental models continue to develop at an amazing rate during this time. For the first time, students begin to question ethics and values. Whose values are right? Whose values are wrong? Why does the *Washington Post* disagree with the *New York Times*? How do I begin to integrate contradicting information? Debates are a highly useful tool for furthering mental models during this time of questioning. Students seem to enjoy and profit from this instructional method. Subconsciously, students realize they need to learn how to examine a variety of perspectives and then decide whether to hold on to, let go of, or change their values, beliefs, and dreams.

Students must be able to examine their own mental models and reflect on the mental models of others. It's crucial for parents, teachers, and students to make a conscious effort to understand and practice the mental models.

Cooperative groups and team building continue to be a valuable educational tool at this level. The teacher is not a guru who has the answer to everything, but a team player who facilitates learning for his/her students. Students have a deeper awareness of the strengths and weaknesses of each other and are able to articulate the process of reaching the end goal, even though diverse perspectives are present.

During the junior high and high school years, students participate in and belong to many clubs. Here they continue to develop the skill of sharing a vision. At the beginning of the year, those who belong to a club must decide what the common goal of the club is for the year. Students must articulate their hopes for the club while listening to what others want and together create a shared vision that everyone is willing to accept and promote.

Obviously, systems thinking continues to grow and develop throughout these years. Students are now able to articulate several complex understandings about a given concept. No longer do they view a situation from one perspective; they view it from multiple perspectives and are able to examine the assumptions and attitudes behind each perspective.

A child's development of these skills does not happen automatically. Parents and teachers must provide the stimuli throughout the child's growing years. In the chapters that follow, we try to give teachers a set of lesson plans that allows them to begin developing these tools with their students. Our lesson plans are simply guidelines, and we encourage teachers to modify them to fit the needs and learning styles of their students. We hope teachers will also share these tools with parents, either through newsletters or during back-to-school nights. We believe if everyone is aware of these tools then miscommunication, misunderstanding, and conflict will soon be extinct.

LESSON PLANS FOR TEACHERS USING PERSONAL MASTERY CONCEPTS

Personal mastery concepts are developmentally appropriate for students in grades 4–12. In this chapter, the reader will find lesson plans for those grades that will assist the teacher in providing opportunities for each student to develop his/her personal mastery skills.

GRADE LEVELS 4–6: LESSON ONE

Multiple Intelligences: verbal/linguistic, interpersonal, intrapersonal

Objectives: Students will be aware of their dreams for their futures. Students will begin to understand the difference between dreams and reality.

Procedure: Ask students to define a dream. Write all ideas on the overhead in a brainstorming session. When all ideas have been given, write a definition that the class will use throughout their work with personal mastery. Ask students for a definition of reality. Once again, write all ideas on the overhead, as you did for the dream brainstorming session. Finally, come up with a definition the class will use throughout the work with personal mastery. Place the two definitions side by side and explore with the class the differences between them. Have the children contribute examples of each to make the definition concrete.

Conclusion: Review the definitions and examples with the students to make sure everyone agrees with/understands what has been written. Place the definitions with the examples at the front of the room so students can consult them as needed.

GRADE LEVELS 4–6: LESSON TWO

Multiple Intelligences: verbal linguistic, interpersonal, intrapersonal

Objective: Students will use definitions of dream and reality to create a visual (poster, collage, or drawing) that illustrates the differences between the two definitions.

Procedure: Give the students these instructions: "Today we are going to use the definitions we wrote yesterday to complete our work. I have put the definitions we agreed upon yesterday on the board for your use. You are to choose two other students to work with on a project today." Once students have formed their groups of three, give the following instructions:

- Each group will complete a visual representation of these definitions by the end of class today.
- Each group will be required to present their visual to the class during tomorrow's session and explain what they did and what it represents.
- Groups may choose to do one of the following: a poster showing the differences between a dream and reality, a collage showing the differences between a dream and reality, or your own drawing showing the differences.

The teacher must make sure she/he has paper, pictures (magazines), and any drawing materials the students may need to complete this project. The teacher should monitor work in the groups and provide feedback to facilitate completion of the assignment.

Conclusion: Students will hang their visual representations on the walls around the room until tomorrow, when they will present them.

GRADE LEVELS 4–6: LESSON THREE

Multiple Intelligences: verbal/linguistic, math/logical, and interpersonal

Objectives: Students will verbalize differences between dreams and reality. Students will present information orally to the class.

Procedure: Students will be asked to share their projects today. Each group will be asked to stand in front of the class and talk about the drawings/collages they have made. Allow all three students to contribute to the presentation by giving them all preparation time with the directive that each must present some of the information to the class. Presentations should be no more than five minutes long. Give the students approximately ten minutes to organize their presentations. Student groups present their drawings/collages to the class. Questions may be asked, and groups should try to answer them.

Conclusion: Students place drawings/collages on the bulletin board under the correct heading (dream or reality).

GRADE LEVELS 4–6: LESSON FOUR

Multiple Intelligences: verbal/linguistic, visual/spatial, interpersonal, bodily/kinesthetic, intrapersonal

Objectives: Students will begin to develop awareness of their personal dreams. Students will begin to use a personal journal.

Procedure: Hand each student a folder in which he or she will complete personal journal assignments. Tell the students they will have time each day to write in their personal journals in order to create a clear picture for themselves of what their dreams are for their future.

Remind the students about the definitions and projects in the front of the room. Remind them that today they are just focusing on dreams. Encourage them to come up to the front of the class, to the bulletin board, if they need help writing.

Assign the first writing topic: "If you asked me today what my dreams are for myself, I would say _____." Let students know they have fifteen minutes to write on this topic today.

Assign the second writing topic: "When I am out of middle school, you could find me doing _____ during the day." Let students know they have fifteen minutes to write today.

Allow students ten minutes at the very end of this class to begin to personalize the outside of their personal journals, as time allows.

Conclusion: Have students choose a partner (or the teacher) to share one idea from their journal writing today.

GRADE LEVELS 4–6: LESSON FIVE

Multiple Intelligences: verbal/linguistic, interpersonal, intrapersonal

Objectives: Students will be aware of goal-setting procedures. Students will use goal-setting procedures to make a goal for the month/semester/year.

Procedure: Begin by saying, "Today we are going to talk about goals. Can anyone tell me what a goal is?" Accept ideas from the students until a complete, working definition is obtained. Once the definition is clear and written on the overhead/board, ask students to think about whether they have any goals at the present moment. Goals do not have to be related to school. A personal example of a goal might get the students off to a good start. Give the students some time to think about goals and then ask them if they are willing to share. Perhaps a think/pair/share process could be used in which the students think, share with another student of their choice, and then share with the whole group. Once students have shared, ask them to take a few minutes to think about the different areas of their lives: school, family, social, extracurricular. Ask students to use their personal journals to write a goal for each area of their lives. These goals can be ones already in existence, or they can be created today.

Conclusion: Review with the class the definition of goals, and discuss briefly the role that goals play in our lives. This lesson can be followed up by the creation of a football field on a bulletin board with goal posts. Students' names can be placed on footballs that can be moved down the field toward completion of their goal. Once they are there, they can make a touchdown!

GOALS: GETTING OFF TO A GOOD START
AREAS TO WORK ON:
FAMILY, SOCIAL, EXTRACURRICULAR
WRITE GOALS IN YOUR JOURNALS

GRADE LEVELS 4–6: LESSON SIX

Multiple Intelligences: verbal/linguistic, interpersonal, bodily/kinesthetic, intrapersonal

Objectives: Students will be aware of how goals relate to personal mastery and conflict resolution. Students will use goals to talk with others about their needs.

Procedure: Today we are going to begin with the work completed yesterday in the personal journals. Ask students to open their journals and take three minutes to remind themselves about what they wrote.

Once students have reminded themselves of their goals, they should be divided into groups of four so they can work cooperatively. Each group will be assigned an area: school, social, family, and extracurricular. Each group will be responsible for creating a skit/role-play to demonstrate to the others in the class not only a goal from their area, but also how they might go about using this goal when a conflict arises.

Give the students the following example: Ted has a goal of completing all homework assignments this quarter. His friends have been begging him to take a night off from doing homework and go with them to a party on a school night. Ted explains to his friends that he has a goal of completing his homework and that if he misses one night he will not achieve the goal. His friends understand the goal, but still want him to go to the party. Ted replies that he is happy to have friends who want him around, but if he doesn't achieve this goal, what might happen for him? He might give up on other goals, he might not get the grade he needs, and so forth.

Students will work with cooperative groups to create the skit/role-play. Monitoring will be necessary, as students may require assistance with some of the planning.

Conclusion: Let students know that skits/role-plays will be performed the next day. Discuss any difficulties that groups had with this process.

GRADE LEVELS 4–6: LESSON SEVEN

Multiple Intelligences: verbal/linguistic, visual/spatial, interpersonal, bodily/kinesthetic, intrapersonal

Objectives: Students will demonstrate ability to use goals to help resolve conflict. Students will provide feedback to others as skits/role-plays are presented.

Procedure: Today we are going to present the skits/role-plays created during yesterday's lesson. Ask for volunteers to present. If no groups volunteer to go first, draw a number from a hat. Those students who are in the audience are asked to watch carefully, as there will be feedback requested at the end of each presentation. Students can use a notebook or paper to take notes if they wish. Students present their skit/role-play. At the end of each skit, ask the audience if they think the outcome of the presentation is realistic. Be sure to elicit specific details that back up the statements made by students in the audience. Thank the students. Proceed this way until all groups have presented.

Conclusion: Discuss with students the value in using their goals to help resolve conflict.

GRADE LEVELS 4–6: LESSON EIGHT

Multiple Intelligences: verbal/linguistic, visual/spatial, interpersonal, intrapersonal

Objective: Students will practice using personal mastery to resolve conflict.

Procedure: Students will be paired to work with a partner. Using either personal journals or newly created scenarios involving conflict, pairs will create a cartoon of eight frames that demonstrates at least two characters involved in a conflict. One character should show personal mastery skills (goal-setting and achievement) to resolve the conflict.

Conclusion: Students will display the cartoons in the area set aside for work on personal mastery. Inform the students that they may look at the cartoons when they are finished with other work.

GRADE LEVELS 4–6: LESSON NINE

Multiple Intelligences: verbal/linguistic, visual/spatial, interpersonal, bodily/kinesthetic, intrapersonal

Objectives: Students will use personal mastery skills to resolve conflict. Students will write a story using personal mastery concepts.

Procedure: Today we are going to write a round robin story. The teacher will start the story with an introductory sentence. Each student is given approximately three minutes to add at least a sentence to what is already written before she/he receives the story. This lesson will take two days to complete. Remind the students that we are using personal mastery/goal setting and achievement to help us resolve conflict. An example of an introductory sentence might be: "Yesterday after school four fifth-grade students were playing ball on the playground when three high school students walked up to them."

While others are creating their pieces to add to the story as it is passed around, the remaining students can work in pairs to create scenarios that might be role-played at a later date to practice the skills they have learned in this unit.

Conclusion: When the story is complete, students can sit in a circle and either have the teacher read the story or pass it around for the students to read parts. A discussion should be facilitated about the story and whether it fulfills the goal of this lesson.

GRADE LEVELS 7–12: LESSON ONE

Multiple Intelligences: bodily/kinesthetic, intrapersonal

Objectives: Students will make a list of their dreams, including areas such as school, home, sports, extracurricular activities, social situations, and careers. Students will consider personal desires/wishes for their future.

Procedure: Tell the students they are going to work individually on what is important to them in their lives, both now and for the future. Help students feel comfortable with this activity by modeling for them some information about your own dreams/desires/wishes for your present life and your future. You might include an achievement for the future (e.g., a new home or having a child). Then turn the discussion to things students might achieve in their current lives or futures. Some examples might be a career, buying a car, living where they want, and having the friends they want.

Encourage students to put aside any fears about what might interfere with reaching these desires/wishes/dreams. Such fears might include what their parents might say about their dreams/wishes. This is just a personal exercise to open up their minds to what they might consider for their futures. Reassure students this is not something carved in stone, but what they envision at this moment in their lives.

Start students out with relaxation/breathing exercises. Have them find someplace comfortable to do some thinking and writing. Remind them the list they are creating includes realities *and* dreams. Set students to work creating the list.

Once students have had time to create (which the teacher should monitor), suggest that the students consider these three questions:

1. What does your dream/achievement look like for you at this moment?
2. What does it feel like when you achieve it? Or when you are working toward it?
3. What are some of the words you might use to describe this achievement?

Once the students have completed the answers, have them go back and make sure that what they have written is really what they want to have happen. Remind them that they need not take into consideration what others, such as their parents, may want for them.

Conclusion: Students should put these personal lists in their folders and be encouraged to ask questions concerning the process or assignment just completed.

GRADE LEVELS 7–12: LESSON TWO

Multiple Intelligences: verbal/linguistic, interpersonal, intrapersonal

Objectives: Students will demonstrate understanding of their current reality. Students will compare/contrast this reality with their dreams.

Procedure: Ask students to take ten minutes to describe in key phrases their current reality. Students write these key phrases on paper. When the time is up, ask students if anyone would like to share. The teacher can begin by sharing, if that helps get the students started. Encourage students to share, even if they share only part of their current reality. The idea is to get everyone involved, and also to get all students to realize the aspects of life that could/should be included when thinking about their current reality. Once the activity is completed, have students use the same paper to write out key phrases to describe their dreams. Have them include career, living circumstances, and so forth. Give them ten minutes. Ask them to share these phrases with the whole group.

After the group sharing, have students each take out a large piece of paper to create a poster/collage. Next, have the students think about their dreams and their realities. In one half of the paper have the students write "Same" and in the second half have them write "Different." They are to then compare and contrast their realities with their dreams by drawing or cutting out pictures that would compare and contrast their realities with their dreams.

Conclusion: Students will hand in their posters/collages for teacher review, not for correct/incorrect work, but so the teacher can ask questions or encourage further thinking.

GRADE LEVELS 7–12: LESSON THREE

Multiple Intelligences: verbal/linguistic and intrapersonal

Objectives: Students will explore their current realities and future dreams for similarities. Students will determine skills/talents necessary for future dreams. Students will determine current personal level of skills/talents.

Procedure: Return the papers from the previous day to the students. Let students know that today they will be working individually. They are to find the similarities on their papers in both the reality and dreams columns. Once the students have determined their similarities based on the same/different activity completed yesterday, they each should write them on a new piece of paper.

Next, students should determine the skills/talents necessary for them to achieve their dreams. This list should be written on the new paper. If necessary, students can work in pairs at this stage to get help with ideas. Teacher should monitor and help as needed. Once the skills/talents have been listed, students should be encouraged to evaluate their present levels for the skills and talents on the list. Perhaps they could use a code system such as a plus sign if they possess a skill, a minus sign if they don't, and a question mark for skills and talents that are in development.

Finally, students should double-check the list to make sure they have listed all skills needed to make their dreams come true.

Conclusion: Collect the papers for today and discuss with students the value of setting personal goals. This goal setting can be done in class during another lesson or on their own.

GRADE LEVELS 7–12: LESSON FOUR

Multiple Intelligences: verbal/linguistic, visual/spatial, interpersonal, intrapersonal

Objectives: Students will reflect upon personal qualities required for future goals/dreams. Students will reflect upon goals/dreams expressed and whether they truly want what has been expressed.

Procedure: Tell the students the work they are going to start will probably require two class periods. Students will be using the work they have already completed on their future goals/wishes/dreams. They are to retrieve their folders and pull out this work to help them answer the following questions suggested by Senge et al. (2000):

1. In your ideal future, you are exactly the kind of person you want to be. What are the qualities you possess?
2. What material things do you own? Describe your ideal living environment.
3. What have you achieved around health, athletics, and anything to do with your body?
4. What is your ideal professional or vocational situation? If you are teaching, in what environment; if not, what are you doing and where?
5. What are you creating for yourself in the arena of individual learning, travel, reading, or other activities?
6. What kind of community or society do you live in?
7. What else, in any other arena of your life, represents the fulfillment of your most desired results?

Once these questions have been answered, students are encouraged to choose someone they trust with whom to share their work. This helps students realize common ground among themselves, which might result in better relationships.

Conclusion: Students should look at what they have written for answers to the above questions. Then they should answer these:

1. If you could have what you have put into your future right now, would you take it?
2. What would the future you envision bring you? What would you get out of it?

GRADE LEVELS 7–12: LESSON FIVE

Multiple Intelligences: verbal/linguistic, visual/spatial, intrapersonal, interpersonal

Objectives: Students will verbalize at least one personal goal. Students will begin to visualize the steps necessary to achieve one of their goals.

Procedure: Talk with students about what goals are. Lead a discussion of students' responses, and write those responses on the overhead while brainstorming. Next, talk with the class about how one goes about achieving a goal one has set: by coming up with an action plan. Draw a staircase on the board/overhead and point out to the students that as we

complete our action plans, we start at the bottom of the stairs and walk up each step in order to reach our goals.

Ask students for a sample goal that they might want to achieve during this school year. Remind them that goals are not just related to school. All aspects of their lives have goals. Once there is a list of goals, choose one, and walk through the steps of the staircase with the students, eliciting ideas about what should be the next step along the way until the top/goal is reached. Explain that each goal has a different number of steps, depending upon factors such as experience, skills, and barriers. Continue the discussion with what might happen if the goal is not accomplished. What would the consequences be? Would failure to the complete the goal affect anything else? Other goals?

Conclusion: Ask students to identify on a handout of a staircase a personal goal they would like to accomplish this year. Then ask them to write the steps they will need to take in order to accomplish the goal. Collect this work at the end of the period.

GRADE LEVELS 7–12: LESSON SIX

Multiple Intelligences: verbal/linguistic, interpersonal, intrapersonal

Objectives: Students will learn to verbalize personal goals. Students will use personal goals to help resolve conflict.

Procedure: Begin with a call for the definition of a conflict. Take students' answers in a brainstorming session until a full description has been obtained. Write the full definition on the overhead/board so all students can see it.

Next, begin a discussion concerning what students currently do to resolve conflict. Again, this is a brainstorming discussion, and there are no wrong answers. Once students have a chance to share current practices, let them know the work the class has been doing on personal mastery will help them to resolve conflicts in some situations. Give the students this example: your friends would like you to go with them to the movies tonight (a school night). You would like to go, but you have a test tomorrow. Your goal is to get good grades to help you get into college, so if you don't study you will not do well and it will affect your grade. You speak up to your friends and tell them that you must study so you can get a good grade on this test and get into college. The truth here should be understood by your friends.

Have the students discuss as a class what might happen with their friends if they face this situation. Would they feel comfortable telling them about the goal of going to college? Would their friends make fun?

Students next get to choose a person to work with for role-playing. They choose a situation that perhaps has happened in the recent past or one they foresee as possible, and they role-play a way to resolve it using personal goals. The partners swap so that each student gets to practice using personal goals to resolve a potential conflict. The teacher should monitor these role-plays, giving feedback as necessary.

Conclusion: Ask the students how the role-plays went. The discussion should evolve around what students said and what the reaction of the peer was. Questions should be answered, and students should be encouraged to practice this use of personal goals to resolve conflicts whenever it is appropriate.

GRADE LEVELS 7–12: LESSON SEVEN

Multiple Intelligences: bodily/kinesthetic, intrapersonal, interpersonal

Objective: Students will use current goals to brainstorm possible conflicts that might arise concerning these goals.

Procedure: Today we are going to examine our personal goals (all areas). Once we have looked over our goals from our personal journals, we are going to list the conflicts that we can think of that might arise as a result of making these goals and trying to achieve them. Students may need some models here:

- Getting to be first string on the basketball team: may have to practice at home and miss out on hanging out with friends.
- Getting into college: may miss hanging out with friends because homework comes first if good grades are to be obtained.
- Dating: may miss out on hanging with friends because of dating.

Once students have had time to brainstorm a list of their own, they may choose a partner with whom to share.

Conclusion: Students will hand in their lists so that ideas can be placed on slips of paper for tomorrow's lesson: practicing role-playing some of these situations.

GRADE LEVELS 7–12: LESSON EIGHT

Multiple Intelligences: verbal/linguistic, visual/spatial, interpersonal, bodily/kinesthetic, intrapersonal

Objective: Students will use personal mastery/goal-setting skills to re-solve conflicts.

Procedure: Prepare for this lesson by creating slips of paper with role-play ideas. These ideas come from the work students completed yesterday. Today, students will use their ideas from yesterday's lesson to role-play solving conflict using their personal mastery skills. Each student will have a chance to be the one to resolve a conflict in a role-play that he or she will choose out of a hat. One at a time, students will choose a slip of paper with a conflict on it. They may also choose the people with whom they need to perform the role-play. The audience decides for each role-play if it meets the requirement of using personal mastery/goal-setting and goal-achieving skills.

Conclusion: Discuss as a class the role-plays and the most difficult part(s) to resolving the conflicts today. Remind the students that these steps are useful for conflicts that occur both inside and outside of school.

GRADE LEVELS 7–12: LESSON NINE

Multiple Intelligences: verbal/linguistic, visual/spatial, interpersonal, bodily/kinesthetic, intrapersonal

Objective: Students will practice using personal mastery to resolve conflict.

Procedure: Students will be paired to work with a partner. Using either personal journals or newly created scenarios involving conflict, pairs will create a cartoon of eight frames that demonstrates at least two characters involved in a conflict. One character should show personal mastery skills (goal setting and achievement) to resolve the conflict.

Conclusion: Students will display the cartoons in the area set aside for work on personal mastery. Students may look at the cartoons when they are finished with other work.

GRADE LEVELS 7–12: LESSON TEN

Multiple Intelligences: verbal/linguistic, visual/spatial, interpersonal, bodily/kinesthetic, intrapersonal

Objective: Students will demonstrate knowledge of personal mastery/goal-setting and goal-achieving skills by creating a poster.

Procedure: Today, students will wind up the unit on personal mastery by creating a poster that displays for others what has been learned. Students divide into groups of four to complete this assignment. Direct the students to use personal journals, cartoons, and any other materials from this unit. Posters should include examples of dreams, goals, and so forth. The final products will be displayed at first in the room and eventually in the halls, to demonstrate one of the many ways conflict can be resolved appropriately. Students may require a brief discussion of major points. Make sure that each member of the group has an assignment (role) if necessary. All members of the group should contribute to the poster in some way.

Conclusion: Hang posters in the room for one week. Students should take the opportunity to view all of the posters before they go on display in the halls of the school.

③

LESSON PLANS FOR TEACHERS USING MENTAL MODELS CONCEPTS

Mental Models

Students in grades K–12 are taught how to recognize mental models and how to develop skills in using the right-hand/left-hand process as well as the ladder of inference. Lesson plans in this chapter provide activities involving songs, plays, puppets, and art that assist the teacher in helping students become proficient users of these skills.

GRADE LEVELS K–3: LESSON ONE

Multiple Intelligences: verbal/linguistic, musical

Objectives: Students will be aware of their thinking processes. Students will begin to gain verbal reasoning skills.

Procedure: The teacher places $5.00 on his/her desk. She/he arranges ahead of time for a student to take the $5.00 off the desk when she/he is out of the room. Later in the day, the teacher inquires, "Did anyone see the $5.00 that was on my desk?" The teacher receives responses such as: "Mary took it," "No, I didn't know it was there," and "I think someone stole it." At this point, the teacher asks someone to describe what everyone might have seen. The responses should be similar to "Mary took the $5.00 off of your desk." The teacher probes the students

with the following questions: "What did you think when you saw Mary take the money?" "Why did you think that way?" The teacher lists the responses on the board and helps the students conclude that even though everyone saw the same action, there are lots of different ways to think about one action. To really understand each other, we need to talk about what we think when we see an action.

Conclusion: Teach this short song (to the tune of "Frere Jacques").

> I see actions
> I see actions
> Then I think
> Then I think
> Everyone thinks differently
> Everyone thinks differently
> It is true
> It is true
>
> Why I think it
> Why I think it
> Say it aloud
> Say it aloud
> Friends will understand me
> Friends will understand me
> It is true
> It is true

GRADE LEVELS K–3: LESSON TWO

Multiple Intelligences: visual/spatial, verbal/linguistic

Objectives: Students will be aware of their thinking processes. Students will begin to gain verbal reasoning skills.

Procedure: Read *The Empty Pot* by Demi to the students. Ask the following questions as you read: What was the Emperor thinking when he decided he needed to choose a successor? How can flowers choose the successor? What were the parents thinking as they hoped their child would be chosen emperor? What was Ping thinking as he planted his

seed? What did Ping think when his seed didn't grow at first? What did
he do to try to help his seed? As all of the children passed Ping with their
flowers, what was Ping thinking? How did Ping feel? What was Ping's father thinking when he looked at Ping's empty pot? What did the Emperor think when he saw Ping's empty pot? What is your favorite part of
the story?

Conclusion: Have the students draw their favorite part of the story.

GRADE LEVELS K–3: LESSON THREE

Multiple Intelligences: visual/spatial, verbal/linguistic, interpersonal

Objectives: Students will be aware of their thinking processes. Students will begin to gain verbal reasoning skills.

Procedure: Each child creates a thinker puppet and gives it a name.
Give each child an empty cardboard roll from wax paper, aluminum foil,
saran wrap, or the like. Tell the students that they are going to create a
"thinker puppet." This puppet will be their very special thinking friend.
As they make their puppets, they have to be able to tell their partner
why they are choosing certain materials. At the end of class, each student has to introduce his/her new friend and share its name. The student must also share why she/he gave it that name.

Conclusion: Introduction of thinker puppets.

GRADE LEVELS K–3: LESSON FOUR

Multiple Intelligences: verbal/linguistic

Objectives: Students will be aware of their thinking processes. Students will begin to gain verbal reasoning skills.

Procedure: Introduce your thinker puppet and explain the puppet's
role: "Hi, class. As you remember, this is Tammy Thinker Puppet. She
has a very special job. There are three questions that Tammy always
asks. The first question is, 'What did you see?' When Tammy asks that,

she wants you to tell her exactly what you saw. Her second question is 'What did you think?' Her last question is 'Why did you think it?' Tammy wants to teach your puppets the same questions. She wants all thinker puppets to be as smart as she is. Put your thinker puppet on your fingers. It's so good to have so many thinker puppets in one place. Tammy, are you ready to begin? Oh, yes. All puppets look at me. You will always ask three questions. The first question is 'What did you see?' All puppets repeat that question. Good! Does any puppet remember what the second question was? Oh, yes—you are right—it is—'What did you think?' All puppets repeat the second question. The third question is 'Why did you think that?' All puppets repeat the third question. Good. Now, let's give our puppets a test."

Walk over to the chalkboard, pick up a piece of chalk, and hold it. Ask the class, "What's the first question your puppet is going to ask—'What did you see?' Yes, that is correct. Can you tell your puppet what you saw." Responses should be similar to "You walked over to the chalkboard and picked up a piece of chalk." Continue saying, "What's the second question your puppet wants to ask—'What did you think?' Correct—these puppets are so smart. Can you tell your puppet what you thought?" Responses should be similar to "I thought you were going to write on the board" or "I thought you were going to hand the chalk to someone so she/he could write on the board." "What great answers!" you respond. "The last question your puppet wants to know is 'Why did you think that?'" Responses should be similar to "Whenever you go to the board and pick up chalk you begin to write" or "Sometimes, you hand chalk to someone so she/he can do math problems."

Conclusion: Finish by saying, "Your puppets are really helping you think well. Remember, whenever you have 'hard thinking' to do, your puppet can help you find the answers."

GRADE LEVELS K–3: LESSON FIVE

Multiple Intelligences: bodily/kinesthetic, verbal/linguistic, interpersonal

Objectives: Students will be aware of their thinking processes. Students will begin to gain verbal reasoning skills.

Procedure: Prepare two students ahead of time to do the following role-play: a student is sitting at his/her desk coloring, when another student walks by and takes the crayon out of the student's hand. Tell the class, "Today, boys and girls, we are going to continue to learn about our thinking. Please take out your thinker puppets, as they will help you. I want you to watch a little play." The students perform the play. After the play, begin a discussion. "What's the first question our thinker puppets want to know? That's right—'What did you see?'" Students should describe the play in their own words. "The second question is—'What did you think?'" Responses will be similar to "I think the child who took the crayon is mean," "I think the child who took the crayon is selfish," "I think the child who took the crayon wants to tease the other person," "I think the teacher wasn't watching very carefully." Those are very good answers. Of course, now our thinker puppets want to know "why did you think that way?" Responses will be similar to "I've heard my mom say people who take things are selfish," "If the teacher had been watching, it wouldn't have happened," or "Sometimes, I like to show someone I like him/her by teasing him/her."

Find a partner. Create a little play just like the one you watched. Be sure you ask your puppets for help in remembering the three questions. We will perform the plays for each other and talk about each of the questions.

Conclusion: Ask the class, "Is everyone finished practicing his/her play? We'll perform the plays and discuss what we see, what we think, and why we think it."

GRADE LEVELS K–3: LESSON SIX

Multiple Intelligences: intrapersonal, interpersonal, verbal/linguistic, musical

Objectives: Students will be aware of their thinking processes. Students will begin to gain verbal reasoning skills.

Procedure: Tell the class, "Today, we are going to choose a picture and write a short story about it. In your story, I want you to tell me what you see in the picture, what you think is happening, and why you think it. We will share our stories with each other."

Conclusion: Share stories and teach this song (to the tune of "Twinkle, Twinkle, Little Star").

> What do I see
> With my eyes?
> What do I think
> As I walk by?
> Why do I think
> That's so clear?
> Different thinking is so dear.
> What do I see
> With my eyes?
> What do I think
> As I walk by?

GRADE LEVELS K–3: LESSON SEVEN

Multiple Intelligences: interpersonal, bodily/kinesthetic

Objectives: Students will be aware of their thinking processes. Students will begin to gain verbal reasoning skills. Students will become aware that sometimes we make predictions before we see what happens.

Procedure: The teacher has twenty-five objects. The students work in pairs. They are to determine whether or not the twenty-five objects will float in water. Before placing each object in a small tub of water, the students must answer the following questions: "What do you think will happen?" and "Why do you think it?" After placing the object in the water, the students will answer the question "What do you see?"

Conclusion: How was our thinking today different from last week?

GRADE LEVELS K–3: LESSON EIGHT

Multiple Intelligences: verbal/linguistic, bodily/kinesthetic, visual/spatial

Objectives: Students will be aware of their thinking processes. Students will begin to gain verbal reasoning skills.

Procedure: Begin by having the students tell the story of "The Three Bears." After the story is told, have the students use their thinker puppets to examine the thinking of each of the main characters. What was Goldilocks thinking as she entered the bears' home? What was she thinking as she tried each bowl of porridge, each chair, and each bed? What were the bears thinking when they left home? What were the bears thinking as they looked at all of the damage Goldilocks had done? What did Goldilocks think when she awoke and found the bears staring at her? What did the bears think as they found Goldilocks?

Conclusion: Tell the students, "Draw a picture of when someone or something surprised you. Write a few sentences telling about what you thought."

GRADE LEVELS K–3: LESSON NINE

Multiple Intelligences: bodily/kinesthetic, visual/spatial, verbal/linguistic

Objectives: Students will be aware of their thinking processes. Students will begin to gain verbal reasoning skills.

Procedure: Give each student a large circle, square, and triangle. On the circle, print the words "What do I see?" On the square, print "What do I think?" On the triangle, print "Why do I think that?" Have the students decorate the shapes however they want. Attach the shapes to a hanger with yarn to create a simple mobile. Hang the mobiles around the classroom to remind students to be aware of their thinking processes.

Conclusion: Discuss with students how often we say things without thinking. If we are aware of our thinking, we will be more careful about what we say and how we say it.

GRADE LEVELS K–3: LESSON TEN

Multiple Intelligences: intrapersonal, interpersonal, visual/spatial, verbal/linguistic

Objectives: Students will be aware of their thinking processes. Students will begin to gain verbal reasoning skills.

Procedure: Create a thinking box for your classroom. Obtain a large refrigerator box. Explain to the students that this box will be used whenever one or two people need to discuss together or think alone about their thinking. For example, out on the playground, sometimes someone gets angry with someone else and calls him/her a name. These two people need to sit in the thinking box and talk about the three questions: (1) What did you see? (2) What were you thinking? and (3) Why were you thinking that? We need to decorate our box. I'm going to divide you into four groups, and each group will get to decorate one side. On the first side, we will put the question "What do you see?" On the second side, we will put the question "What did you think?" And on the third side, we will put the question "Why did you think it?" The fourth side will have the words to the songs we've learned to help us remember how to think about our thinking.

Conclusion: Discuss situations in which the box may be used.

GRADE LEVELS 4–6: LESSON ONE

Multiple Intelligences: verbal/linguistic

Objectives: Students will be aware of their thinking processes. Students will begin to gain verbal reasoning skills. Students will become aware of their own viewpoints. Students will begin to accept others' viewpoints.

Procedure: Read the following story to the students.

Once upon a time, there was a town where all of the citizens were blind. The older people told their children frightening stories about a monster who lived in the forest just outside of the village. Most people were afraid to go into the forest, for fear of being attacked by the ferocious beast.

One day, three leaders of the city decided to go into the forest together to find out whether or not the stories were true. Together, they walked into the forest, and eventually they located an elephant, who was grazing contentedly on a tree.

Now, the three men were blind, so they couldn't see the "monster." One of the blind men reached out and grabbed the elephant's ear. Another touched and felt the elephant's trunk. And the third took hold of one of the elephant's feet and legs. Armed with the information they could gather about the creature in this way, they went back home.

When they returned to the town, the three men called all the villagers around them. The townspeople were eager to hear a description of the creature that had created such fear. The first man, who had felt the elephant's ear, said "I put my hands on the creature, and I can tell you what it is. It is a large, rough thing, wide and broad, like a carpet.

The second man, who had felt the elephant's trunk, broke in. "No," he cried, "I laid my hands on the creature, and I can tell you what it is. It is like a straight and hollow pipe."

Then the third man, who touched the feet and legs, said, "Both of you are wrong. I laid my hands on the creature, and I can tell you what it is. It is mighty and firm like a pillar." (Adapted from *World Tales*, by Idries Shah)

Discussion questions: Why did each of the three men describe the elephant so differently? Was each of the three men correct in his description? Is it possible that the three men could have had a big argument over who was right? How would you have settled their argument?

Divide the class into two groups. Have one half of the class stand on one side of the room and the other half of the class stand on the opposite side of the room. Stand in the middle of the classroom. Hold up a T-shirt that has a picture on one side and writing on the other side. Ask one student who can see only the front of the T-shirt to describe what she/he sees. Then ask a student who can see only the opposite side to describe what she/he sees. Next, ask the class who is correct. When students respond that both students are correct, ask how this is possible. Discuss with the students how people generally assume that their perspective is always correct and that the other person's must be wrong. In reality, both perspectives are correct. We need to remember that, when we are in conflict, we need to step back and try to see what the other person might be seeing.

Conclusion: Have students give examples of situations in which two different perspectives are present.

GRADE LEVELS 4–6: LESSON TWO

Multiple Intelligences: verbal/linguistic, visual/spatial, interpersonal, intrapersonal

Objectives: Students will be aware of their thinking processes. Students will begin to gain verbal reasoning skills. Students will begin to use the right-hand/left-hand column tool.

Procedure: Often, when we talk to people, we aren't fully aware of what we are thinking. Today, we are going to learn about a tool that can assist us in understanding our conversations. The name of this tool is the right-hand/left-hand column. Have the students take a sheet of paper and fold it long ways. At the top of the first column have them put the words "Left-Hand Column," and at the top of the second column, have them put the words "Right-Hand Column." Underneath the left-hand column, have them write "What I'm Thinking," and below the right-hand column, have them write "What Is Said."

Now, let's look at the conversation between Jay and Bill (see table 3.1). What might Jay have been thinking as he asked Bill to come over?

Possible thoughts:

- No one is going to be home tonight, and I don't want to be home alone.
- Bill is so smart and always does what he's supposed to. Maybe I can get him in trouble.
- Bill is my best friend, and I just want to spend some time with him.

Table 3.1. The Left-Hand/Right-Hand Column

Left-Hand Column	Right-Hand Column
What I'm Thinking	What Is Said
	J: Hey, Bill, come on over to my house, and we'll shoot some hoops.
	B: I can't. I have to do my homework first.
	J: Are you a nerd? Who does homework? I never do it?
	B: I guess I can do it later. I'll be right over.

Now, let's look at what Bill might have been thinking as he responded to Jay.

Possible thoughts:

- My parents' rule is I must do my homework before I go out. I don't want to argue with them.
- I get better grades if I do my homework earlier rather than later.

Again, let's look at what Jay might have been thinking as he responded to Bill.

Possible thoughts:

- I really don't want to be alone. Maybe if I call him a name, he'll change his mind.
- It's time that Bill knows what everyone else is calling him, so I'll call him a nerd.

Let's look at the thoughts behind Bill's final response to Jay.

Possible thoughts:

- I would rather argue with my parents than have Jay think I'm a nerd.
- I can still do my assignment, it just won't be as good as usual, and I'm doing OK in that class, anyway.

So often in our conversations, we respond to each other unaware of what we are really thinking. Sometimes during conversations, we say things we don't really mean because we are hurt or angry. The right-hand column/left-hand column tool allows us to reflect on our own thoughts. You really can't do a left-hand column for the person you're talking to.

Have the students practice this new technique by having each do one by him/herself. Instruct the students to "Think of a short argument you had with someone. Write the argument in the right-hand column. In the left-hand column, write what you were thinking as you responded. Don't worry about what the other person was thinking. Only write your thoughts."

Conclusion: Have each student share his/her argument and thoughts with one other person in the class.

GRADE LEVELS 4–6: LESSON THREE

Multiple Intelligences: verbal/linguistic, visual/spatial, interpersonal, intrapersonal, bodily/kinesthetic

Objectives: Students will be aware of their thinking processes. Students will begin to gain verbal reasoning skills. Students will begin to use the right-hand/left-hand column tool.

Procedure: Divide the students into groups of four. Assign the following roles: two main characters and a "thinker" for each main character. Give each group a scenario. First, the group must write out the right-hand column—what's said. Next, the students will work in pairs. One of the main characters and his/her thinker will discuss what she/he is thinking as the conversation is occurring. The other main character and his/her thinker will do the same.

After practicing, the groups will perform the scenarios for each other. The thinker will insert the character's thoughts after each part of the dialogue.

Possible scenarios:

- Your parents have set a ten o'clock curfew for you on Friday nights. You want to stay out later this Friday.
- You want to have friends sleep over and mom doesn't think it's a good idea.
- Your friend wants you to smoke a cigarette. You really don't want to do this.
- You overheard John call your best friend a "nerd." You tell John to stop doing this.
- You and your best friend are shopping. Your friend dares you to take something without paying for it.
- At recess, your best friend asks you to let him copy off of you during the history test because she/he didn't have time to study.
- Your mom asks you to clean up your room and you really don't want to do it.

- The teacher knows you know who took $50 out of her purse. She asks you to tell her who did it.

Conclusion: Say to the students, "As you watched the scenarios, what did you learn about how people think? How does knowing what a person is thinking help you understand him/her better?"

GRADE LEVELS 4–6: LESSON FOUR

Multiple Intelligences: verbal/linguistic, visual/spatial, interpersonal, intrapersonal

Objectives: Students will be aware of their thinking processes. Students will begin to gain verbal reasoning skills. Students will be introduced to the ladder of inference.

Procedure: The ladder of inference is a mental model construct that we use daily. Instruct the students on the different steps on the ladder. Step 1 is asking "What are the observable data in this classroom?" Answers may be desks, books, chalkboard, windows, doors, students, teachers, and so on. It's very important to remember that observable data is factual. Step 2 on the ladder is "I add meaning to the data." Based on past experiences, knowledge, and personality, we give meaning to everything we see. Illustrate this with an example: "Doug and David are best friends. They go everywhere together. One day, I see Doug with Andy, and David isn't around. I immediately think Doug and David had a fight and aren't friends anymore. Who can tell me what the observable data are? That's right! Doug and David are always together. Doug is with Andy, and David isn't around. Who can tell what meaning I added? Correct! Doug and David had a fight and aren't friends anymore. Step 3 of the ladder is to ask myself 'How did you arrive at that conclusion?' Once I had a best friend and we had a fight, and now we both have new friends, so I assume that that's what has happened with Doug and David."

We make inferences so many times each day. Some of our inferences are correct, and some are incorrect. Our inferences always seem correct from our perspective—it's when the inference is viewed from a different perspective that it might seem incorrect.

Have the students do one more scenario: "See if you can pick out the observable data, the meaning I added, and what might have helped you reach that conclusion. All the students are taking a history test. I see Sue reach in her pocket, take out a small scrap of paper, unfold it, look at it, refold it, put it back in her pocket, and write an answer down. I decide Sue is cheating.

"What's the observable data? All students are taking a history test. Sue reaches in her pocket, takes out a scrap of paper, unfolds it, reads it, refolds it, puts it back in her pocket, and writes an answer down.

"What meaning did I add? Sue is cheating.

"What helped me add that meaning?

- My mother taught me about 'crib sheets.'
- My friends have shown me their 'crib sheets.'
- Sue has a reputation for being dishonest.

"Is it possible to add another meaning? If so, what is it, and what helps you add that meaning?"

Conclusion: Ask the students to think about an action they saw today. What were the observable data? What meaning did they add? Why did they add that meaning? Have each student share his/her thoughts with a partner.

GRADE LEVELS 4–6: LESSON FIVE

Multiple Intelligences: verbal/linguistic, interpersonal, intrapersonal, bodily/kinesthetic

Objectives: Students will be aware of their thinking processes. Students will begin to gain verbal reasoning skills. Students will practice using the ladder of inference.

Procedure: Say to the students, "Yesterday, we learned about the ladder of inference. Who remembers what the three steps are? That's right. Step 1 is 'What are the observable data?' Step 2 is 'What meaning did I add?' And step 3 is 'Why did I add that meaning?' Today, you are going to work in cooperative learning groups. I want each group to create a skit. In your skit, you must have observable data and add meaning to it. Your group needs to brainstorm why that particular meaning might be added. You will perform your skits for each other, but don't tell why that meaning was added—we'll let the rest of the class figure it out, and you can tell them if they are correct." After each group performs its skit, discuss the following three questions:

1. What were the observable data?
2. What meaning was added?
3. Why did I add that meaning?

Conclusion: Have the students continue to use this process throughout their day.

GRADE LEVELS 4–6: LESSON SIX

Multiple Intelligences: verbal/linguistic, interpersonal, intrapersonal, bodily/kinesthetic

Objectives: Students will be aware of their thinking processes. Students will begin to gain verbal reasoning skills. Students will practice using the ladder of inference.

Procedure: Today, the students are going to work in groups. Each group will choose one person to be "Captain Thinker." Captain

Thinker's role is to ask three questions: What were the observable data? What meanings were added? and Why did I add those meanings? All members of the group are to create a skit in which two people get into an argument. The arguments should be real ones that have happened to someone in the group in the past. After the argument, Captain Thinker will ask the three questions to each person who was arguing. After each person has answered the questions, the group will help the two find a solution for the argument.

Conclusion: Share skits and solutions with the entire class.

GRADE LEVELS 4–6: LESSON SEVEN

Multiple Intelligences: visual/spatial, musical, intrapersonal

Objectives: Students will make a visual to help them remember the ladder of inference. Students will learn a song to help them remember the ladder of inference.

Procedure: Create a ladder of inference mobile. Give students a ladder of inference pattern or let them create their own ladder. Have them draw it on light tagboard and decorate the ladder anyway they choose. Be sure the students ask the three questions (1) What are the observable data? (2) What meaning did I add? and (3) Why did I add that meaning? on the correct steps.

Teach the following song (to the tune of "This Land Is Your Land"):

> Reflective Thinking
> Reflective Thinking
> Begins with seeing and then add meaning
> From life experiences to our knowledge base
> Reflective thoughts are a part of me.

Conclusion: Students will show their ladders to their classmates. The teacher will display the ladders in the classroom.

GRADE LEVELS 4–6: LESSON EIGHT

Multiple Intelligences: interpersonal, visual/spatial, verbal/linguistic

Objective: Students will practice using the ladder of inference.

Procedure: Each student is to work with a partner. Each pair is to create a four-panel cartoon illustrating the ladder of inference.

Conclusion: Display cartoons around the room.

GRADE LEVELS 4–6: LESSON NINE

Multiple Intelligences: verbal/linguistic and interpersonal

Objective: Students will practice using the ladder of inference.

Procedure: Briefly retell the following fairy tales:

- Snow White and the Seven Dwarfs
- Little Red Riding Hood
- Cinderella
- Beauty and the Beast

Have each group choose one of the fairy tales. Each group should take a scene from the fairy tale and look at the actions of the main character. Walk through the ladder of inference questions with that character—if the answers lead the group to rewrite that scene, encourage students to do so.

Conclusion: Share the fairy tales with the entire class.

GRADE LEVELS 4–6: LESSON TEN

Multiple Intelligences: interpersonal, bodily/kinesthetic, intrapersonal, verbal/linguistic

Objective: Students will practice using the ladder of inference.

Procedure: Divide students into groups. Have each group create a skit teaching other fourth to sixth graders how to use the ladder of inference.

Conclusion: Perform the skits for another class.

GRADE LEVELS 7–12: LESSON ONE

Multiple Intelligences: verbal/linguistic

Objectives: Students will be aware of their thinking processes. Students will begin to gain verbal reasoning skills. Students will become aware of their own viewpoints. Students will begin to accept others' viewpoints.

Procedure: Read the following story to the students.

Once upon a time, there was a town where all of the citizens were blind. The older people told their children frightening stories about a monster who lived in the forest just outside of the village. Most people were afraid to go into the forest, for fear of being attacked by the ferocious beast.

One day, three leaders of the city decided to go into the forest together to find out whether or not the stories were true. Together they walked into the forest, and eventually they located an elephant, who was grazing contentedly on a tree.

Now, the three men were blind, so they couldn't see the "monster." One of the blind men reached out and grabbed the elephant's ear. Another touched and felt the elephant's trunk. And the third took hold of one of the elephant's feet and legs. Armed with the information they could gather about the creature in this way, they went back home.

When they returned to the town, the three men called all the villagers around them. The townspeople were eager to hear a description of the creature that had created such fear. The first man, who had felt the elephant's ear, said, "I put my hands on the creature, and I can tell you what it is. It is a large, rough thing, wide and broad, like a carpet."

The second man, who had felt the elephant's trunk, broke in. "No," he cried, "I laid my hands on the creature, and I can tell you what it is. It is like a straight and hollow pipe."

Then the third man, who touched the feet and legs, said, "Both of you are wrong. I laid my hands on the creature, and I can tell you what it is. It is mighty and firm like a pillar." (Adapted from *World Tales*, by Idries Shah)

Discussion Questions: Why did each of the three men describe the elephant so differently? Was each of the three men correct in his description? Is it possible that the three men could have had a big argument over who was right? How would you have settled their argument?

Divide the class into two groups. Have one half of the class stand on one side of the room and the other half of the class stand on the opposite side of the room. Stand in the middle of the classroom. Hold up a T-shirt that has a picture on one side and writing on the other side. Ask one student who can see only the front of the T-shirt to describe what she/he sees. Then ask a student who can see only the opposite side to describe what she/he sees. Next, ask the class who is correct. When students respond that both students are correct, ask how this is possible. Discuss with the students how people generally assume that their perspective is always correct and that the other person's must be wrong. In reality, both perspectives are correct. We need to remember that, when we are in conflict, we need to step back and try to see what the other person might be seeing.

Conclusion: Have students give examples of situations in which two different perspectives are present.

GRADE LEVELS 7–12: LESSON TWO

Multiple Intelligences: verbal/linguistic, visual/spatial, interpersonal, intrapersonal

Objectives: Students will be aware of their thinking processes. Students will begin to gain verbal reasoning skills. Students will begin to use the right-hand/left-hand column tool.

Procedure: Often, when we talk to people, we aren't fully aware of what we are thinking. Today, we are going to learn about a tool that

Table 3.2. The Left-Hand/Right-Hand Column

Left-Hand Column	Right-Hand Column
What I'm Thinking	What Is Said
	J: Hey, Bill, come on over to my house, and we'll shoot some hoops.
	B: I can't. I have to do my homework first.
	J: Are you a nerd? Who does homework? I never do it?
	B: I guess I can do it later. I'll be right over.

can assist us in understanding our conversations. The name of this tool is the right-hand/left-hand column. Have the students take a sheet of paper and fold it long ways. At the top of the first column, have them put the words "Left-Hand Column," and at the top of the second column, have them put the words "Right-Hand Column." Underneath the left-hand column, have them write "What I'm Thinking," and below the right-hand column have them write "What Is Said."

Now, let's look at the conversation between Jay and Bill (see table 3.2). What might Jay have been thinking as he asked Bill to come over? Possible thoughts:

- No one is going to be home tonight, and I don't want to be home alone.
- Bill is so smart and always does what he's supposed to. Maybe I can get him in trouble.
- Bill is my best friend, and I just want to spend some time with him.

Now, let's look at what Bill might have been thinking as he responded to Jay.

Possible thoughts:

- My parents' rule is I must do my homework before I go out. I don't want to argue with them.
- I get better grades if I do my homework earlier rather than later.

Again, let's look at what Jay might have been thinking as he responded to Bill.

Possible thoughts:

- I really don't want to be alone. Maybe if I call him a name, he'll change his mind.
- It's time that Bill knows what everyone else is calling him, so I'll call him a nerd.

Let's look at the thoughts behind Bill's final response to Jay.
Possible thoughts:

- I would rather argue with my parents than have Jay think I'm a nerd.
- I can still do my assignment, it just won't be as good as usual, and I'm doing OK in that class, anyway.

So often in our conversations, we respond to each other unaware of what we are really thinking. Sometimes during conversations, we say things we don't really mean because we are hurt or angry. The right-hand column/left-hand column tool allows us to reflect on our own thoughts. You really can't do a left-hand column for the person you're talking to.

Have the students practice this new technique by having each do one by him/herself. Instruct the students to "Think of a short argument you had with someone. Write the argument in the right-hand column. In the left-hand column, write what you were thinking as you responded. Don't worry about what the other person was thinking. Only write your thoughts."

Conclusion: Have each student share his/her argument and thoughts with one other person in the class.

GRADE LEVELS 7–12: LESSON THREE

Multiple Intelligences: verbal/linguistic, visual/spatial, interpersonal, intrapersonal, bodily/kinesthetic

Objectives: Students will be aware of their thinking processes. Students will begin to gain verbal reasoning skills. Students will begin to use the right-hand/left-hand column tool.

Procedure: Divide the students into groups of four. Assign the following roles: two main characters and a "thinker" for each main character. Give each group a scenario. First, the group must write out the right-hand column—what's said. Next, the students will work in pairs. One of the main characters and his/her thinker will discuss what she/he is thinking as the conversation is occurring. The other main character and his/her thinker will do the same. After practicing, the groups will perform the scenarios for each other. The thinker will insert the character's thoughts after each part of the dialog.

Possible scenarios:

- Your parents have set a twelve o'clock curfew for you on Friday nights. You want to stay out later this Friday.
- You want to have a party for about fifty of your friends, and mom doesn't think it's a good idea.
- Your friend wants you to try crack. You really don't want to do this.
- You overheard John call your best friend a "nerd." You tell John to stop doing this.
- You and your best friend are shopping. Your friend dares you to take something without paying for it.
- Between classes, your best friend asks you to let him copy off of you during the history test because she/he didn't have time to study.
- Your mom asks you to clean up your room and you really don't want to do it.
- The teacher knows you know who took $50 out of her purse. She asks you to tell her who did it.

Conclusion: Say to the students, "As you watched the scenarios, what did you learn about how people think? How does knowing what a person is thinking help you understand him/her better?"

GRADE LEVELS 7–12: LESSON FOUR

Multiple Intelligences: verbal/linguistic, visual/spatial, interpersonal, intrapersonal

Objectives: Students will be aware of their thinking processes. Students will begin to gain verbal reasoning skills. Students will be introduced to the ladder of inference.

Procedure: The ladder of inference is a mental model construct that we use daily. Instruct the students of the different steps on the ladder. Step 1 is "What are the observable data in this classroom?" Answers may be desks, books, chalkboard, windows, doors, students, teachers, and so on. It's very important to remember that observable data are factual. Step 2 on the ladder is "I add meaning to the data." Based on past experiences, knowledge, and personality, we give meaning to everything we see. Illustrate this with an example: "Doug and David are best friends. They go everywhere together. One day, I see Doug with Andy, and David isn't around. I immediately think Doug and David had a fight and aren't friends anymore. Who can tell me what the observable data are? That's right! Doug and David are always together. Doug is with Andy, and David isn't around. Who can tell what meaning I added? Correct! Doug and David had a fight and aren't friends anymore. Step 3 of the ladder is to ask myself 'How did you arrive at that conclusion?' Once I had a best friend and we had a fight and now we both have new friends, so I assume that that's what has happened with Doug and David."

We make inferences so many times each day. Some of our inferences are correct, and some are incorrect. Our inferences always seem correct from our perspective—it's when the inference is viewed from a different perspective that it might seem incorrect.

Have the students do one more scenario: "See if you can pick out the observable data, the meaning I added and what might have helped me reach that conclusion. All the students are taking a History test. I see Sue reach in her pocket, take out a small scrap of paper, unfold it, look at it, refold it, put it back in her pocket, and write an answer down. I decide Sue is cheating.

"What's the observable data?

"All students are taking a history test. Sue reaches in her pocket, takes out a scrap of paper, unfolds it, reads it, refolds it, puts it back in her pocket, and writes an answer down.

"What meaning did I add?

"Sue is cheating.

"What helped me add that meaning?

- My mother taught me about 'crib sheets.'
- My friends have shown me their 'crib sheets'
- Sue has a reputation for being dishonest.

"Is it possible to add another meaning? If so, what is it, and what helps you add that meaning?"

Conclusion: Have the students think about an action they saw today. What were the observable data? What meaning did they add? Why did they add that meaning? Have each student share his/her thoughts with a partner.

GRADE LEVELS 7–12: LESSON FIVE

Multiple Intelligences: verbal/linguistic, interpersonal, intrapersonal, bodily/kinesthetic

Objectives: Students will be aware of their thinking processes. Students will begin to gain verbal reasoning skills. Students will practice using the ladder of inference.

Procedure: Say to the students, "Yesterday, we learned about the ladder of inference. Who remembers what the three steps are? That's right. Step one is 'What are the observable data?' Step two is 'What meaning did I add?' And Step three is 'Why did I add that meaning?' Today, you are going to work in cooperative learning groups. I want each group to create a skit. In your skit, you must have observable data and add meaning to it. Your group needs to brainstorm why that particular meaning might be added. You will perform your skits for each other, but don't tell why that meaning was added—we'll let the rest of the class figure it out and you can tell them if they are correct." After each group performs its skit, have them discuss the following three questions:

1. What were the observable data?
2. What meaning was added?
3. Why did I add that meaning?

Conclusion: Have the students continue to use this process throughout their day.

GRADE LEVELS 7–12: LESSON SIX

Multiple Intelligences: verbal/linguistic, intrapersonal, interpersonal

Objectives: Students will be aware of someone using the ladder of inference. Students will articulate the incorrect conclusions drawn from "climbing the ladder."

Procedure: Show a clip of the film *Shrek*, beginning with the scene in which Donkey is in the cave with Fiona, and Shrek overhears the conversation. Stop the video when Shrek finishes his conversation with Donkey. Use the following questions to begin a discussion:

- What conclusions did Shrek draw?
- What steps in the ladder of inference did Shrek skip in order to draw those conclusions?
- What past experiences helped Shrek draw those conclusions?
- Do donkey and Fiona know why Shrek is angry? Why not?

Have each student work with a partner. Each one is to share a story that is similar to the one they just watched.

Conclusion: Have a couple of students share their stories with the entire class. Have the class discern which of the steps were skipped and brainstorm ways of how not to "climb the ladder" so quickly.

GRADE LEVELS 7–12: LESSON SEVEN

Multiple Intelligences: verbal/linguistic, intrapersonal, interpersonal

Objectives: Students will be aware of someone using the ladder of inference. Students will articulate the incorrect conclusions drawn from "climbing the ladder."

Procedure: Divide students into pairs. Give each pair an interview from a current magazine. Have students complete the following process:

1. Read the interview. One of you should be the interviewee and the other the interviewer. Highlight one section in which you can determine that either the interviewer or the interviewee "climbed the ladder of inference."
2. Discuss with your partner the key concepts that led you to this conclusion.
3. How would you rewrite the section so that the "ladder of inference" doesn't come into play?

Conclusion: Have each pair share their information with one other pair in the class.

GRADE LEVELS 7–12: LESSON EIGHT

Multiple Intelligences: interpersonal, bodily/kinesthetic, intrapersonal, verbal/linguistic

Objective: Students will practice using the ladder of inference.

Procedure: Divide students into groups. Have each group create a skit teaching other seventh to twelfth graders how to use the ladder of inference.

Conclusion: Perform the skits for another class.

GRADE LEVELS 7–12: LESSON NINE

Multiple Intelligences: interpersonal, visual/spatial, verbal/linguistic

Objective: Students will practice using the ladder of inference.

Procedure: Each student is to work with a partner. Each pair is to create a twelve-panel cartoon illustrating the ladder of inference.

Conclusion: Display cartoons around the room.

GRADE LEVELS 7–12: LESSON TEN

Multiple Intelligences: interpersonal, intrapersonal, verbal/linguistic

Objective: Students will practice using the ladder of inference.

Procedure: Choose one of the wars. List the causes of the war. Create a skit involving a person who wants to go to war and one who does not. Include in your skit at least two instances in which one of the persons uses the ladder of inference. Lead a short class discussion and see if the class can pick out the examples that were in your skit.

Conclusion: Discuss how being aware of the ladder of inference keeps fights from escalating.

4

LESSON PLANS FOR TEACHERS USING SHARED VISION CONCEPTS

Shared vision concepts are developmentally appropriate for students in grades 3–12. This chapter is filled with group activities that will assist students in learning how to use effective listening and speaking skills to create a shared vision.

GRADE LEVELS 3–6: LESSON ONE

Multiple Intelligences: intrapersonal, interpersonal, visual/spatial, mathematical/logical

Objective: The students will create a shared vision through determining classroom rules and consequences.

Procedure: The teacher and the students will discuss how students learn and what type of rules are needed to create a positive environment. Students and teacher will brainstorm the consequences of breaking these rules. All will agree upon four to five rules and on the consequences for breaking each rule. The students will be divided into groups, each of which will create a poster stating one of the rules and the consequence for breaking it. These posters may be decorated in an attractive manner. They will be hung in the classroom for the entire year.

Conclusion: Each group will share its poster with the entire class, reading the rule and consequence and explaining any symbols the group has used.

GRADE LEVELS 3–6: LESSON TWO

Multiple Intelligences: interpersonal, intrapersonal, musical/rhythmic, verbal/linguistic

Objective: The students will create a class song.

Procedure: The teacher and students will brainstorm ideas on how students would like to be treated throughout the year. Following this discussion, the students and teacher will talk about goals they would like to accomplish as a class this year—perhaps they want to be "buddies" for kindergartners or for elderly people in the nursing home. Perhaps they want to focus on saving the earth by sponsoring different earth literacy projects for their school. After brainstorming, the class will vote on two to three ideas that it would like to implement. Students are divided into pairs and asked to create a song that contains the ideas they brainstormed.

Conclusion: Students will perform songs for each other.

GRADE LEVELS 3–6: LESSON THREE

Multiple Intelligences: verbal/linguistic, intrapersonal, interpersonal, visual/spatial, bodily/kinesthetic

Objective: Students will use maxims to recognize shared vision concepts.

Procedure: Explain that in our life there are many maxims, sayings, or adages that are used that denote a shared vision. Have the students divide into groups of four. Give each group a list of adages. Each group is to select two adages and discuss the meaning of each. During the discussion, the students will also talk about how each applies to their lives. They are to create a skit in which each adage is used.

Maxims, sayings, adages:

- Opportunity knocks but once.
- Kill two birds with one stone.
- Don't cry over spilt milk.
- Actions speak louder than words.
- Don't put all of your eggs in one basket.
- You can lead a horse to water but you can't make him drink.
- Birds of a feather will flock together.
- Age is like love, it cannot be hid.
- Well begun is half done.
- Every beginning is hard.
- If the blind lead the blind, both shall fall into a ditch.

- If at first you don't succeed, try, try again.
- A stitch in time saves nine.
- What goes around comes around.
- You can't fool mother nature.
- A bird in the hand is worth two in the bush.
- A rolling stone gathers no moss.
- Handsome is as handsome does.
- Home is where the heart is.
- Take some time to smell the roses.
- Do unto others as you would have them do unto you.
- Absence makes the heart grow fonder.
- Out of sight, out of mind.
- Don't judge a book by its cover.

Conclusion: Students will perform skits for each other.

GRADE LEVELS 3–6: LESSON FOUR

Multiple Intelligences: verbal/linguistic, interpersonal

Objective: Students will create a shared vision using an ordinary object.

Procedure: Students are placed in cooperative learning groups. They will use their knowledge and social skills to determine the answers to the questions below. The teacher will have a group of ordinary objects in a bag. A member from each group will select one object from the bag without looking. Each group will look at their object for a few moments. The teacher will ask the questions below, giving groups time to respond between each question. When the group has agreed on the answer, they will write it down.

1. What animal does your object remind you of?
2. Describe two ways in which your animal is beautiful.
3. Name three reasons why people like your animal.
4. Give two ways you love and respect your animal.
5. Describe two ways you can help your animal feel important and needed.

Conclusion: Have each group share its information. Students should explain what their object was and how they came up with the answers to the questions. After their presentations, follow-up discussion should focus on how groups created positive descriptions for an inanimate object and the process used to reach agreement.

Sample list of objects: paper clip, key, napkin, pencil, cup, roll of tape.

GRADE LEVELS 3–6: LESSON FIVE

Multiple Intelligences: interpersonal, verbal/linguistic

Objective: Students will work as a team in developing a shared vision.

Procedure: The teacher will place the students in cooperative learning groups. Each group will complete the following statements:

If I weren't me, I would like to be a (an) _____.
The reason I want to be a (an) _____ is _____.

Each group must agree with whatever is chosen. Each team member must be able to give a reason for the choice.

Example: If I weren't me, I would like to be a prism. The reason I want to be a prism is that it reflects light and makes beautiful patterns on the walls. Another reason I would like to be a prism is that the sun shining through me would warm me.

Conclusion: Each group will share its sentences and reasons with its classmates.

GRADE LEVELS 3–6: LESSON SIX

Multiple Intelligences: interpersonal, verbal/linguistic, bodily/kinesthetic, visual/spatial

Objective: Students will work as a team to develop a shared vision.

Procedure: Divide students into cooperative learning groups. Each group is to create a new game for reviewing material covered in class.

Each group must agree on the title of the game and the rules for playing it. Give each group a sheet of poster board. The students are to write the title of the game and the rules. Each group will teach the rest of the class how to play its game. Students will play the new games.

Conclusion: Discuss the process of creating the game with the class. Was it difficult to agree on the rules? How did you decide, as a group, what to include and what to exclude? Was it difficult to write the rules so everyone would understand them? How does this experience reflect a "shared vision?"

GRADE LEVELS 3–6: LESSON SEVEN

Multiple Intelligences: verbal/linguistic, intrapersonal, interpersonal, mathematical/logical, bodily/kinesthetic

Objective: Students will work as a team to develop a shared vision.

Procedure: Give each student a worksheet divided into three columns. The first column is labeled "nouns," the second column is labeled "verbs," and the third column is labeled "adjectives." Review with the students what nouns, verbs, and adjectives are. Read a short fairy tale to the students. As you read, the students are to write at least five words in each column. When you are finished reading, ask each student to write a sentence using the words in the columns. The students do not have to use all of the words. After each student has completed the task, put the students into groups of four. Each group is to create a fairy tale that uses all four sentences. Of course, they can add other sentences to the story.

Conclusion: Have the students perform fairy tales for each other. Once again, ask the students about the process. How did they arrive at their story? How did they decide who would play which part?

GRADE LEVELS 3–6: LESSON EIGHT

Multiple Intelligences: intrapersonal, interpersonal, visual/spatial, mathematical/logical, verbal/linguistic

Objective: Students will work as a team to develop a shared vision.

Procedure: Students are to individually design their own country. The country's name must be part of the student's name. For example, if a student is named Ann, her country's name might be Annalusia. After each student has completed his/her country, students should be grouped in fours. Each group of four needs to take the four countries and create a continent. Each group needs to name its continent. Students should add rivers, mountains, and so forth to the continents. After all the groups have created continents, the entire class should to work together to create a "world." The world map should be placed on the wall. Students should create ten geography questions using the world map.

Conclusion: Each student exchanges his/her geography questions with another student. Each student answers the questions and hands the questions and answers in to the teacher.

GRADE LEVELS 3–6: LESSON NINE

Multiple Intelligences: intrapersonal, interpersonal, mathematical/ logical, verbal/linguistic

Objective: Students will work as a team to develop a shared vision.

Procedure: Students should get back into their "continent groups." They are to "create" the people who live on their continents. What type of features will the people have? What type of body shapes will they have? What color eyes and hair will be predominant? After they have discussed the physical features of their population, they must create a language for their people to speak. They must first create an alphabet and then create simple phrases. The alphabet should be logical, so that anyone can learn it and use it. Each group should write a one-paragraph story using its new language. They should write the story in the roman alphabet, rather than in the one they have created, so others can decipher the story.

Conclusion: Each group rotates to the right and reads and deciphers the story created in the "new language."

GRADE LEVELS 3–6: LESSON TEN

Multiple Intelligences: mathematical/logical, interpersonal, visual/spatial

Objective: Students will work as a team to develop a shared vision.

Procedure: Students are placed in their continent groups again. Each group is to design its continent's economic system. Will the people have a money system like that of the United States, or will they have a barter system? If they choose to create a "money system," coins and paper money should be designed. The students will need to decide how much each coin is worth and create a table with the amounts. If they choose to create a barter system, they should create a table showing the base of the bartering (e.g., two chickens may be traded for five pounds of sugar).

Conclusion: Each group should share its economic system with the whole class. If time allows, the teacher might begin instruction on currency exchange and then have the class develop exchange rates between continents.

GRADE LEVELS 7–12: LESSON ONE

Multiple Intelligences: intrapersonal, interpersonal, visual/spatial, mathematical/logical

Objective: The students will create a shared vision through determining classroom rules and consequences.

Procedure: The teacher and the students will discuss how students learn and what type of rules are needed to create a positive environment. Students and teacher will brainstorm the consequences of breaking these rules. All will agree upon four to five rules and the consequences for breaking each rule. The students will be divided into groups, each of which will create a poster stating one of the rules and the consequence for breaking it. These posters may be decorated in an attractive manner. They will be hung in the classroom for the entire year.

Conclusion: Each group will share its poster with the entire class, reading the rule and consequence and explaining any symbols the group might have used.

GRADE LEVELS 7–12: LESSON TWO

Multiple Intelligences: interpersonal, intrapersonal, musical/rhythmic, verbal/linguistic

Objective: The students will create a class mascot and song.

Procedure: The teacher and students will brainstorm ideas on how students would like to be treated throughout the year. Following this discussion, the students and teacher will talk about goals they would like to accomplish as a class this year—perhaps they want to be "buddies" for kindergartners or for elderly people in the nursing home. Perhaps they want to focus on saving the earth by sponsoring different earth literacy projects for their school. After brainstorming, the class will vote on two to three ideas it would like to implement. Students are divided into pairs and asked to create a song that contains the ideas they brainstormed. After creating the song and reflecting on the goals they have decided upon, the students will create a mascot for their class.

Conclusion: Students will perform songs for each other.

GRADE LEVELS 7–12: LESSON THREE

Multiple Intelligences: verbal/linguistic, intrapersonal, interpersonal, visual/spatial, bodily/kinesthetic

Objective: Students will use maxims to recognize shared vision concepts.

Procedure: Explain that in our life there are many maxims, sayings, or adages that are used that denote a shared vision. Divide students into groups of four. Give each group a list of adages. Each group is to select two adages and discuss the meaning of each. During the discussion, the students will also talk about how each applies to their lives. They are to create a skit in which each adage is used.

Maxims, sayings, adages:

- Opportunity knocks but once.
- Kill two birds with one stone.
- Don't cry over spilt milk.
- Actions speak louder than words.
- Don't put all of your eggs in one basket.
- You can lead a horse to water but you can't make him drink.
- Birds of a feather will flock together.
- Age is like love, it cannot be hidden.
- Well begun is half done.
- Every beginning is hard.
- If the blind lead the blind, both shall fall into a ditch.
- If at first you don't succeed, try, try again.
- A stitch in time saves nine.
- What goes around comes around.
- You can't fool mother nature.
- A bird in the hand is worth two in the bush.
- A rolling stone gathers no moss.
- Handsome is as handsome does.
- Home is where the heart is.
- Take some time to smell the roses.
- Do unto others as you would have them do unto you.
- Absence makes the heart grow fonder.
- Out of sight, out of mind.
- Don't judge a book by its cover.

Conclusion: Students will perform skits for each other.

GRADE LEVELS 7–12: LESSON FOUR

Multiple Intelligences: verbal/linguistic, interpersonal

Objective: Students will create a shared vision using an ordinary object.

Procedure: Students are placed in cooperative learning groups. They will use their knowledge and social skills to determine the answers to the questions below. The teacher will have a group of ordinary objects in a bag. A member from each group will select one object from the bag without looking. Each group will look at their object for a few moments. The teacher will ask the questions below, giving groups time to respond between each question. When the group has agreed on the answer, they will write it down.

1. What animal does your object remind you of?
2. Describe two ways in which your animal is beautiful.
3. Name three reasons why people like your animal.
4. Give two ways you love and respect your animal.
5. Describe two ways you can help your animal feel important and needed.

Conclusion: Have each group share its information. The group should explain what its object was and how the students came up with the answers to the questions. After the presentations, follow-up discussion should focus on how the group created positive descriptions for an inanimate object and the process used to reach agreement.

Sample list of objects: paper clip, key, napkin, pencil, cup, roll of tape.

GRADE LEVELS 7–12: LESSON FIVE

Multiple Intelligences: interpersonal, verbal/linguistic

Objective: Students will work as a team in developing a shared vision.

Procedure: The teacher will place the students in cooperative learning groups. Each group will complete the following statement:

If I weren't me, I would like to be a (an) _____.
The reason I want to be a (an) _____ is _____.

Each group must agree with whatever is chosen. Each team member must be able to give a reason for the choice.

Example: If I weren't me, I would like to be a prism. The reason I want to be a prism is that it reflects light and makes beautiful patterns on the walls. Another reason I would like to be a prism is that the sun shining through me would warm me.

Conclusion: Each group will share its sentences and reasons with classmates.

GRADE LEVELS 7–12: LESSON SIX

Multiple Intelligences: interpersonal, verbal/linguistic, bodily/kinesthetic, visual/spatial

Objective: Students will work as a team to develop a shared vision.

Procedure: Divide students into cooperative learning groups. Each group is to create a new game for reviewing material covered in class. The game cannot be similar to one seen on television. Each group must agree on the title of the game and the rules for playing it. Give each group a sheet of poster board. The students are to write the title of the game and the rules. Each group will teach the rest of the class how to play its game. Students will play the new games.

Conclusion: Discuss the process of creating the games with the class. Was it difficult to agree on the rules? How did you decide as a group what to include and what to exclude? Was it difficult to write the rules so everyone would understand them? How does this experience reflect a "shared vision"?

GRADE LEVELS 7–12: LESSON SEVEN

Multiple Intelligences: verbal/linguistic, intrapersonal, interpersonal, mathematical/logical, bodily/kinesthetic

Objective: Students will work as a team to develop a shared vision.

Procedure: Give each student a worksheet divided into three columns. The first column is labeled "nouns," the second column is labeled "verbs," and the third column is labeled "adjectives." Review with the students what nouns, verbs, and adjectives are. Read a short section of literature to the students. As you read, the students are to write at least five words in each column. When you are finished reading, ask each student to write a sentence using the words in the columns. All of the words do not have to be used. After each student has completed the task, put the students into groups of four. Students are to create a fairy tale that uses all four sentences. Of course, students can add other sentences to the story.

Conclusion: Students perform fairy tales for each other. Once again, ask the students about the process. How did they arrive at their story? How did they decide who would play which part?

GRADE LEVELS 7–12: LESSON EIGHT

Multiple Intelligences: verbal/linguistic, intrapersonal, interpersonal, visual/spatial

Objective: Students will work as a team to develop a shared vision.

Procedure: Students will watch the first half hour of the film *Shrek*. Divide students into cooperative learning groups. Each group should discuss examples of shared vision that they saw. Which characters shared "a vision"? Was it freely chosen or forced upon them? Discuss two other movies students have recently seen and how shared vision is depicted in them.

Conclusion: Students are to be observant of human behavior for the rest of the day. How often do they witness the "shared vision" concept?

GRADE LEVELS 7–12: LESSON NINE

Multiple Intelligences: verbal/linguistic, intrapersonal, interpersonal

Objective: Students will work as a team to develop a shared vision.

Procedure: Students will decide on a service learning project to do together. Students will brainstorm possible activities that will help those in need. After the large group has brainstormed a number of possibilities, students are divided into cooperative groups. Each group will brainstorm advantages and disadvantages for each activity. When the groups are finished, the teacher will conduct a whole group discussion of advantages and disadvantages for each activity. The class will arrive at a decision on which activity to pursue through the consensus process.

Conclusion: The entire class will participate in the service learning project.

GRADE LEVELS 7–12: LESSON TEN

Multiple Intelligences: verbal/linguistic, intrapersonal, interpersonal, visual/spatial, bodily/kinesthetic

Objective: Students will work as a team to develop a shared vision.

Procedure: Divide the students into cooperative learning groups. Students will create two skits. The first skit will depict the essential qualities for developing a shared vision. The second skit will depict a team planning process in which the shared vision model fails. Members of the audience are to determine which of the two scenes was presented, and a short discussion should follow.

Conclusion: Students are to write a three-paragraph essay on the values of shared vision.

LESSON PLANS FOR TEACHERS FOR TEAM BUILDING ACTIVITIES

Team Learning
(Cooperative Learning)

Students in grades 4–12 may be taught team building skills. Shared vision and team-building skills are so interconnected that it is difficult to cleanly separate them. This chapter is filled with group activities that continue to develop the shared vision skills while focusing on team-building skills. Students have a myriad of group opportunities to develop these skills as they participate in the suggested activities found in this chapter.

GRADE LEVELS 4–6: LESSON ONE

Multiple Intelligences: intrapersonal, interpersonal, visual/spatial, verbal/linguistic

Objectives: The students will learn the roles in cooperative learning groups. The students will work together to create a story using personal experiences.

Procedure: The teacher will place students into cooperative learning groups of four. Each student will be assigned a role: leader, recorder, materials handler, or reader. Each group will create a story using personal experiences. The topic of the story is "A Friend in Need is a Friend Indeed." Students are to complete the following steps:

1. The materials handler will go to the front table to retrieve paper, markers, and colored pencils.
2. The leader will help the group in a discussion of the personal experiences of each member concerning a friend who has needed help.
3. The recorder will write the key ideas from each experience on the paper with the markers.
4. The reader will read to the group the ideas shared by members of the group.
5. The group will work together to create characters for the story and a problem that one of the characters had. (The leader facilitates and the recorder writes.)
6. The group will use the ideas shared to help create both the characters and the problem. (The leader facilitates and the recorder writes.)

7. The group will then write a story using the characters, details about the problem, and details about the way the problem was handled. (The leader facilitates and the recorder writes.)

Conclusion: Final copies of the stories from the groups are printed and shared with the class.

GRADE LEVELS 4–6: LESSON TWO

Multiple Intelligences: intrapersonal, interpersonal, verbal/linguistic, visual/spatial, mathematical/logical

Objective: The students will use cooperative learning groups to create a "machine" that will solve a local, national, or global problem.

Procedure: The teacher will assign students to cooperative learning groups of four, with the following roles: recorder, data collector, materials handler, and leader. Groups will then work together to brainstorm a list of problems at the local, national, or global level. If the groups have trouble getting started, the teacher may need to stop the group session and hold a large class brainstorming session. Sample topics might include:

- Local county landfill expansion
- School budget crisis
- Terrorism around the globe

Once the list has been recorded, the groups should each choose a problem. That problem is recorded and another brainstorming session begins for deciding what kind of "machine" might be used to solve this problem. The materials handler must then retrieve the materials necessary for creating a "machine" that could be used to solve the problem. Students are instructed, "Remember: the only limits to what you design are what you make!" Meanwhile, the rest of the group should be accessing resource materials (texts, online, etc.) to help them accurately detail what the "machine" will do and how. The data collector will record these data.

This plan could take several days to complete. At the end of the first session, students in each group will be asked to share their progress with the class and ask for feedback. This procedure will be followed on subsequent days until projects/"machines" are complete.

Conclusion: When the "machines" are complete, they will be displayed in the class, and students will have a chance to visit each during their free time.

GRADE LEVELS 4–6: LESSON THREE

Multiple Intelligences: verbal/linguistic, interpersonal, intrapersonal, bodily/kinesthetic, visual/spatial

Objective: The students will work with a partner to complete an assignment.

Procedure: Students will be assigned a partner with whom to complete an assignment. Once partners have been assigned, students are to choose which one will draw and which will give the directions for what will be drawn. The student who gives the directions cannot move any body parts but his/her mouth. The student drawing may only draw and may not ask questions.

Students should be given the following directions before beginning this assignment: "You are about to learn what it takes to really have to think before you speak and really listen to what a speaker is saying. You are going to work with a partner to complete a drawing assignment. One of you will give directions; the other will listen to the directions and follow them. The person giving the directions will be given a drawing/picture that his/her partner will draw when given directions. This means the person giving the directions must be sure that the directions are clear and easy to follow. The person doing the drawing, that is, following the directions, must be sure to listen carefully. The person drawing may not speak and the person giving the directions may not help draw or make any motion for what is to be drawn."

In each pair, the student giving the instructions is handed a picture. Students are given the remainder of the class period to complete the drawing.

Conclusion: Students will hand in the picture and the drawing completed in class. The following day, class will start with a discussion of this experience.

GRADE LEVELS 4–6: LESSON FOUR

Multiple Intelligences: visual/spatial, verbal/linguistic, bodily/kinesthetic, interpersonal, mathematical/logical

Objective: Students will use cooperative learning groups to design a new toy.

Procedure: Instruct the class as follows: "Today we are going to work in groups and put your creativity to work. You are going to work together in your groups to design something new for the toy market. You may not duplicate something already on the market, but you may change something in a way to make it work better or faster." The teacher may need to brainstorm ideas for the groups.

Each member of the group must participate in the project. The group must come up with a finished drawing and a scaled model. Each group will have time in class tomorrow to present its design and scaled model to the rest of the class.

Conclusion: Groups will hand in their designs and models to the teacher to be stored until tomorrow. The teacher will remind the groups that tomorrow's class will begin with the presentations.

GRADE LEVELS 4–6: LESSON FIVE

Multiple Intelligences: verbal/linguistic, bodily/kinesthetic, interpersonal, intrapersonal, visual/spatial

Objective: Students will use cooperative learning groups to create an updated version of a popular fairy tale.

Procedure: The teacher will need to have on hand several copies of popular fairy tales that the students may use in their groups. Students will be assigned groups of three to four to work together to create an updated version of the fairy tales. Groups will be given copies of the fairy tale of their choice. The teacher will give the following directions:

- Your job today is to reread the fairy tale and decide what changes you would like to make to update the story.
- Characters, plot, and setting are the best places to start.
- Include details to enrich your fairy tales.
- You may include illustrations with your updated fairy tale if you wish.
- Each person in your group must contribute to the finished product.
- When the fairy tales are completed, we will post them in the room, and I will give you time during the next week to look at them and read them if you wish.

Conclusion: Groups will hand in their fairy tales to be posted around the room.

GRADE LEVELS 4–6: LESSON SIX

Multiple Intelligences: verbal/linguistic, bodily/kinesthetic, interpersonal, intrapersonal, musical/rhythmic

Objective: Students will use cooperative learning groups to create a song.

Procedure: The teacher will have available tape recorders and blank cassettes for student use for this project. Students will be assigned to groups of three to four. Once the groups have been assigned, students will be given these directions:

- Today, we are going to work in these groups to create a song. Each group will be asked to come up with the lyrics (words) for its song and either create its own music or use music the group members are familiar with as the melody.
- Each member of the group must contribute to the project.

- You will be asked to present this final song to the class, either in person or on tape.
- You will be required to hand in your written lyrics and a tape of your song.
- Your song does not have to be a long one, as it may be similar to children's songs you have learned.

The teacher should monitor the work of the groups, making sure to answer any questions and provide support for this process.

Conclusion: Groups will hand in both the lyrics and their tapes to the teacher. Tapes may be used tomorrow for the presentations.

GRADE LEVELS 4–6: LESSON SEVEN

Multiple Intelligences: verbal/linguistic, visual/spatial, interpersonal, intrapersonal

Objectives: The students will work as a cooperative learning team to complete a project of their choice. The students will use their cooperative learning groups to choose roles and divide the work to complete the project.

Procedure: Instruct the class as follows: "Today, you are all going to get some choice in what work you complete over the next three days. You will number off from one to four and meet with your group. A list of projects you may choose from will then be placed on the overhead. Each group may choose its own project based on group consensus."

Here you may need to have a conversation with the class about what "consensus" means. This process should include an equal opportunity for each member of the group to voice his/her opinion about the project preferred. If the choices cannot be agreed upon unanimously, the group members will discuss the advantages and disadvantages of each project preferred. Then a vote will be taken. Whatever project the majority votes for is the one the group will complete.

Once the project has been chosen, then members of the group must work together to decide upon roles. This process should include strengths of the individual members in a discussion. Once the strengths have been listed and discussed, each member should choose a role and the group should concur.

Projects might include:

1. Research on a variety of topics from the science or social studies areas.
2. Completion of a book the group would present to either another group or to students in another grade.
3. A series of illustrations to be presented on paper, on poster board, or in power point on the history of a sport of interest.
4. Creation of an invention that the group is interested in drawing the schematics for and actually creating in at least scale form.

Conclusion: Students will present their projects to members in the class. Each member of the group must participate in this oral presentation.

GRADE LEVELS 4–6: LESSON EIGHT

Multiple Intelligences: verbal/linguistic, interpersonal, intrapersonal, bodily/kinesthetic

Objective: The students will use cooperative learning skills to solve a social problem.

Procedure: The lesson starts with the teacher asking the entire class to brainstorm a list of social situations/problems that either have occurred or that they have seen. (Students should feel free to contribute after the sessions on "checking in.") The teacher should be prepared to contribute social situations as needed: a friend wants to borrow your homework because she/he didn't get hers/his done, the bully wants you to pay her/him $1.00 every day to leave you alone, and so forth.

Students are then allowed to choose their own groups of three to four. Each person in the class must be included in the choosing. Students will not be assigned roles, but will work together following the rules of checking in to solve their problem.

Students in each group will discuss which problem they would like to solve until the group votes and comes to some consensus. Once the problem is chosen, the group must work together, with each member given a chance to be heard, to find a solution. The members of the group must be in consensus on the solution. One member of the group may volunteer to record the steps to the solution.

Conclusion: Once the groups have completed their work, they will each give an oral presentation to the entire class, with each member of the group participating, on their problem and its solution.

GRADE LEVELS 4–6: LESSON NINE

Multiple Intelligences: verbal/linguistic, interpersonal, intrapersonal, bodily/kinesthetic

Objectives: The students will use cooperative learning groups to solve a state-level problem. The students will work cooperatively so each member of the group is valued.

Procedure: Instruct the students as following: "Today, we will begin a two-day lesson in which you will work in groups to solve a problem that affects not only you, but the entire state. We will begin today by brainstorming a list of possible state problems." Students can contribute ideas while the teacher writes these on the board or overhead. Remember that these ideas should be state-level focus. Also, you may have to feed the students an idea or two to get things started. Some sample starters might be:

- Drought
- Unemployment

Once the class has come up with a list that they feel is comprehensive for their needs, the class will discuss, with teacher facilitation, each of the problems on the list. Students will be encouraged to take their own notes as the teacher jots notes for each problem on the overhead or board. This discussion should include items such as who is impacted, in what way, and for how long. At the end of this discussion, the class will vote for the problem they are most interested in trying to solve.

On day two, students should be assigned to their groups and given roles. Once this has been done, each group will address the problem from its own perspective, trying to solve it. Once again, the concept of each member of the group being heard is important (checking-in concept). A member of each group will serve as recorder, but all members will orally present the solution the group arrives at. Groups may use visual aids to present their solutions.

Conclusion: Each group will orally present its solution to the class's chosen problem.

GRADE LEVELS 4–6: LESSON TEN

Multiple Intelligences: verbal/linguistic, interpersonal, intrapersonal, bodily/kinesthetic, visual/spatial

Objectives: The students will use cooperative learning groups to teach either a skill or information to another group.

Procedure: Instruct the class as follows: "Today, we are not only going to learn something new, but we are also all going to be teachers." Students are assigned to learning groups. Once assigned, the groups must each decide on either a skill to teach or information to share with another group(s). A brief class discussion should take place both to define skills and determine what kind of information might be shared. Once again, the members are to listen to each other and value what has been shared by each member (this is the "checking-in" concept). Once the group has shared ideas and discussed the advantages and disadvantages of each, its members are to come to consensus.

Each group will be given the rest of the class period to work on the steps to teaching the skill or sharing the information. Each member of the group must be involved in the presentation.

Students in the group may need supplies such as paper, markers, crayons, overhead transparencies, and PowerPoint equipment.

Conclusion: Students will teach their lessons tomorrow in class.

GRADE LEVELS 7–12: LESSON ONE

Multiple Intelligences: intrapersonal, interpersonal, visual/spatial, verbal/linguistic

Objectives: The students will learn the roles in cooperative learning groups. The students will work together to create a story using personal experiences.

Procedure: The teacher will place students into cooperative learning groups of four. Each student will be assigned a role: leader, recorder, materials handler, or reader. Each group will create a story using personal experiences. The topic of the story is "A Friend in Need Is a Friend Indeed." Students are to complete the following steps:

1. The materials handler will go to the front table to retrieve paper, markers, and colored pencils.
2. The leader will help the group in a discussion of the personal experiences of each member concerning a friend who has needed help.
3. The recorder will write the key ideas from each experience on the paper with the markers.
4. The reader will read to the group the ideas shared by members of the group.
5. The group will work together to create characters for the story and a problem that one of the characters had. (The leader facilitates and the recorder writes.)
6. The group will use the ideas shared to help create both the characters and the problem. (The leader facilitates and the recorder writes.)
7. The group will then write a story using the characters, details about the problem, and details about the way the problem was handled. (The leader facilitates and the recorder writes.)

Conclusion: Final copies of the stories from the groups are printed and shared with the class.

GRADE LEVELS 7–12: LESSON TWO

Multiple Intelligences: intrapersonal, interpersonal, verbal/linguistic, visual/spatial, mathematical/logical

Objective: The students will use cooperative learning groups to create a "machine" that will solve a local, national, or global problem.

Procedure: The teacher will assign students to cooperative learning groups of four, with the following roles: recorder, data collector, materials handler, and leader. Groups will then work together to brainstorm a list of problems at the local, national, or global level. If the groups have trouble getting started, the teacher may need to stop the group sessions and hold a large class brainstorming session. Sample topics include:

- Local county landfill expansion
- School budget crisis
- Terrorism around the globe

Once the list has been recorded, the groups should each choose a problem. That problem is recorded and another brainstorming session begins for deciding what kind of "machine" might be used to solve this problem. The materials handler must then retrieve the materials necessary for creating a "machine" that could be used to solve the problem. Students are instructed, "Remember: the only limits to what you design are what you make!" Meanwhile, the rest of the group should be accessing resource materials (texts, online, etc.) to help them accurately detail what the "machine" will do and how. The data collector will record these data.

This plan could take several days to complete. At the end of the first session, students in each group will be asked to share their progress with the class and ask for feedback. This procedure will be followed on subsequent days until projects/"machines" are complete.

Conclusion: When the "machines" are complete, they will be displayed in the class, and students will have a chance to visit each during their free time.

GRADE LEVELS 7–12: LESSON THREE

Multiple Intelligences: verbal/linguistic, musical, visual/spatial, interpersonal, bodily/kinesthetic, intrapersonal

Objectives: The students will explore "dialogue" as used in team building. The students will learn/use the process of "checking in."

Procedure: Instruct the class as follows: "Today, we are going to begin a series of lessons on team building. In order for all of us to work better as a team, we are going to begin with practicing how to 'dialogue.' To start each class over the next few days, we are going to learn to check in. This means that each of us will get one minute to speak about what we are thinking, what we are feeling, or what we have noticed. The focus of what we will be speaking about will be our personal experience."

Stress to the students the value of speaking from personal experience. The students can choose what they wish to contribute during this "check-in." Some might just say, "I am here." Others may talk about the latest events in their lives. It really doesn't matter, as long as everyone speaks to the whole group. Students who are shy or not ready to participate in the check-in can "pass," but they are required to say this aloud. This will give students practice in listening to what others are saying without having to make a response. Full focus can be placed on what is being said.

It might be best if the teacher goes first to set the stage for what can be expected. She/he can choose from these possibilities as examples for starting:

"I am here."
"I have had a great morning of teaching thus far!"
"I have had a hard time getting my students to pay attention this morning."

Once the teacher has started, there are typically two patterns followed: going around the circle in one direction and allowing each student to speak in turn or allowing students to speak in any order, as they feel comfortable. Check-ins are safe ways for students to speak up about what is on their minds. Students should feel as though they can express whatever feelings they are experiencing and be accepted by the class.

Once all of the students have checked in, the teacher leads a brief discussion around what just occurred during check-in. The teacher should be looking for students to talk about what they experienced while they listened to all of the others. How was this experience different from others they have had? How was this different from a normal two-person conversation?

Conclusion: Remind students that the lessons for the next few days will be on team building and that today's lesson will be used to start each day, at least for the next day or two.

GRADE LEVELS 7–12: LESSON FOUR

Multiple Intelligences: verbal/linguistic, interpersonal, intrapersonal, bodily/kinesthetic

Objective: The students will use cooperative learning skills to solve a social problem.

Procedure: The lesson starts with the teacher asking the entire class to brainstorm a list of social situations/problems that either have occurred or that they have seen. (Students should feel free to contribute after the sessions on "checking in.") The teacher should be prepared to contribute social situations as needed: a friend wants to borrow your homework because she/he didn't get hers/his done, the bully wants you to pay her/him $1.00 every day to leave you alone, and so forth.

Students are then allowed to choose their own groups of three to four. Each person in the class must be included in the choosing. Students will not be assigned roles, but will work together following the rules of checking in to solve their problems.

Students in each group will discuss which problem they would like to solve until the group votes and comes to some consensus. Once the problem is chosen, the group must work together, with each member given a chance to be heard, to find a solution. The members of the group must be in consensus on the solution. One member of the group may volunteer to record the steps to the solution.

Conclusion: Once the groups have completed their work, they will each give an oral presentation to the entire class, with each member participating, on their problem and its solution.

GRADE LEVELS 7–12: LESSON FIVE

Multiple Intelligences: verbal/linguistic, interpersonal, intrapersonal, bodily/kinesthetic

Objectives: The students will use cooperative learning groups to solve a national-level problem. The students will work cooperatively so each member of the group is valued.

Procedure: Instruct the students as following: "Today we will begin a two-day lesson in which you will work in groups to solve a problem that affects not only you, but the entire nation. We will begin today by brainstorming a list of possible national problems." Students can contribute ideas while the teacher writes these on the board or overhead. Remember that these ideas should be national-level focus. Also, you may have to feed an idea or two to get things started. Some sample topics might be:

- Federal budget/social programs
- National unemployment

Once the class has come up with a list that it feels is comprehensive for its needs, the class will discuss, with teacher facilitation, each of the problems on the list. Students will be encouraged to take their own notes as you jot notes for each problem on the overhead or board. This discussion should include items such as who is impacted, in what way, and for how long? At the end of this discussion, the class will vote for the problem they are most interested in trying to solve.

On day two, students should be assigned to their groups and given roles. Once this has been done, each group will address the problem from its own perspective, trying to solve it. Once again, the concept of each member of the group being heard is important (checking-in concept). A member of each group will serve as recorder, but all members will orally present the solution the group arrives at. Groups may use visual aids to present their solutions.

Conclusion: Each group will orally present its solution to the class's chosen problem.

GRADE LEVELS 7–12: LESSON SIX

Multiple Intelligences: verbal/linguistic, interpersonal, intrapersonal

Objective: Students will use cooperative learning groups to create a survey for their fellow students.

Procedure: Instruct the class as follows: "Today, we are going to work together in groups to create a survey that you will give to fellow students. You will be asked as a group to come up with a topic you think needs to be addressed, choosing either from among school issues or social issues. Then you will create a list of questions that you will type out and we will print once we have edited it. You will hand this survey out to other students to complete. Once the survey is complete, you will look at the results as a group and come up with some conclusions. You will present these conclusions to the class." The teacher may need to brainstorm with the students to come up with a list of possible topics for school issues, which may include:

- Off-campus lunch
- Study hall requirements
- Elective classes offered

Possible topics as social issues might be:

- Drinking and driving
- Drug use
- Age for driver's license

Conclusion: Students will hand in their typed versions of surveys for teacher approval. The teacher will then arrange for surveys to be completed by fellow students. Once the surveys are complete, students will report findings to the class.

GRADE LEVELS 7–12: LESSON SEVEN

Multiple Intelligences: verbal/linguistic, interpersonal, intrapersonal, bodily/kinesthetic, visual/spatial

Objective: Students will use cooperative learning groups to complete an obstacle course.

Procedure: The teacher will have to make arrangements to use the gym or other outside facilities for this lesson. She/he may also want to solicit input from the PE teacher about student abilities. Students will work in cooperative groups to complete an obstacle course. Each team will have five members, who must all participate in part of the course. Before each group takes its turn on the course, it should sit together and come up with a strategy for using all of its members to achieve the best possible time. The teacher should monitor group discussions and provide support whenever necessary.

Conclusion: When all groups have been through the obstacle course, the teacher should facilitate a discussion on the process used to determine which members participated in which parts of the course. The focus of the discussion should be on the necessity to complete the work using all members.

GRADE LEVELS 7–12: LESSON EIGHT

Multiple Intelligences: verbal/linguistic, interpersonal, intrapersonal, bodily/kinesthetic, visual/spatial

Objective: Students will use cooperative learning groups to create a detailed map and directions to another place in the school.

Procedure: Instruct the students as follows: "Today, we are going to put your map and group skills to work. You will choose your own groups of three to four to complete the work we will do. Let me tell you what you are to accomplish by the end of the class period."

- Each group will be required to make a detailed set of steps or directions to be followed to get from this classroom to another place in our building or on the grounds.
- Each group will be required to complete a detailed map and a key for the directions that are to be followed.
- Each member of the group must participate in the completion of the project.

Once students have chosen their group members, the teacher should hand out paper and any other supplies deemed necessary by the groups to complete their projects. She/he should monitor the group work and make suggestions as needed.

Conclusion: Students hand in completed maps and directions to the teacher. Tomorrow, each group will be given a list of directions not of their creation to follow. Once the directions have been followed and the groups have returned, the teacher will hand out maps to determine the accuracy of both steps and maps.

GRADE LEVELS 7–12: LESSON NINE

Multiple Intelligences: verbal/linguistic, interpersonal, intrapersonal, mathematical/logical, visual/spatial

Objective: Students will use cooperative learning groups to participate in a math bowl competition.

Procedure: Make a set of math questions appropriate for the level of students in the class. These questions should span all areas taught to date in math, with questions varying in level of thinking skills needed to answer them. For example, one question might be a straightforward three-step word problem using addition, multiplication, and division. Another question might require the use of geometry (shape knowledge). A third might require the use of a calculator to complete a graph. The teacher will place students in four cooperative groups or teams. Give the following directions:

- Today we are going to have a math bowl. You will be assigned to the following teams. . . .
- Once the teams have moved to sit together, members should discuss strengths in math.
- Once strengths have been discussed, areas of difficulty should also be discussed so that each member may be encouraged to use his/her strengths to participate.
- All members of the team must answer at least one question in the bowl.
- Teams will be given twenty seconds to answer each question. If a team is unable to answer, another team may buzz in to try to answer the question. The team with the most points at the end is the winner.

The teacher will facilitate questions for the bowl, making sure to vary level and type of question.

Conclusion: A prize of the teacher's choice will be awarded to the team who wins. Also, the teacher should facilitate a discussion about the process for the member participation on each team.

Note: The example above is math, but this plan could be used with any subject area.

GRADE LEVELS 7–12: LESSON TEN

Multiple Intelligences: verbal/linguistic, visual/spatial, interpersonal, intrapersonal

Objectives: The students will work as a cooperative learning team to complete a project of their choice. The students will use their cooperative learning groups to choose roles and divide the work to complete the project.

Procedure: Instruct the class as follows: "Today, you are all going to get some choice in what work you complete over the next three days. You will number off from one to four and meet with your group. A list of projects you may choose from will then be placed on the overhead. Each group may choose its own project based on group consensus."

Here you may need to have a conversation with the class about what "consensus" means. This process should include an equal opportunity for each member of the group to voice his/her opinion about the project preferred. If the choices cannot be agreed upon unanimously, the group members will discuss the advantages and disadvantages of each project preferred. Then a vote will be taken. Whatever project the majority votes for is the one the group will complete.

Once the project has been chosen, then members of the group must work together to decide upon roles. This process should include strengths of the individual members in a discussion. Once the strengths have been listed and discussed, each member should choose a role and the group should concur.

Projects might include:

1. Research and presentation on a career/vocation of interest to members of the group. This could be either on poster board or in PowerPoint.
2. Research on a variety of topics from the science or social studies areas.
3. Completion of a book the group would present to either another group or to students in another grade.
4. A series of illustrations to be presented on paper, on poster board, or in PowerPoint on the history of a sport of interest.
5. Creation of an invention that the group is interested in drawing the schematics for and actually creating. The group will be asked to demonstrate this invention for the class.

Conclusion: Students will present their projects to members in the class. Each member of the group must participate in this oral presentation.

6

LESSONS FOR TEACHERS FOR USING SYSTEMS THINKING CONCEPTS

Systems Thinking

Graphic organizers are the foundational skills for developing systems thinking. This chapter contains lesson plans for grades K–12. Students will have the opportunity to use a variety of graphic organizers in the primary grades. Middle school and high school students will quickly review graphic organizers and move into systems thinking activities.

GRADE LEVELS K–3: LESSON ONE

Multiple Intelligences: visual/spatial, verbal/linguistic, bodily/kinesthetic

Objectives: Students will become familiar with a Venn diagram. Students will be able to sort colors.

Procedure: The teacher places two hula hoops on the floor so they intersect. The teacher has seven red objects, seven yellow objects, and seven objects that have both red and yellow on them. The teacher places the word "red" above one hula hoop and the word "yellow" above the other hula hoop. The teacher holds up one object and asks where it belongs. The teacher calls on a student and asks him/her to put it in the right place. After each object is placed, the teacher questions the student as to why she/he chose to place it in that particular spot.

Conclusion: Each child is given a Venn diagram worksheet. Each student is asked to choose two colors and create a Venn diagram using those colors.

GRADE LEVELS K–3: LESSON TWO

Multiple Intelligences: visual/spatial, musical/rhythmic, interpersonal, intrapersonal, mathematical/logical

Objectives: Students will remember the sequence of a song. Students will create a story board using "The Farmer in the Dell."

Procedure: The teacher begins by having the class sing "The Farmer in the Dell." After the singing is finished, the teacher asks the students to list the order of the people, animals, or things as each was called into the circle. After the students have orally given the teacher the order, the students are placed in cooperative learning groups and given large chart paper. Each group is to draw in correct sequence the order that occurs in the song.

Conclusion: Groups will share their chart drawings with the whole class.

GRADE LEVELS K–3: LESSON THREE

Multiple Intelligences: mathematical/logical, interpersonal, bodily/kinesthetic

Objectives: Students will listen to a story and be able to retell it in correct sequence. Students will use a chain-of-events graphic organizer.

Procedure: The teacher will read the story of "The Three Bears." After reading the story, the teacher will hand out the worksheet (see figure 6.1). The students will cut the strips apart and paste them in correct sequence, making a chain. Each strip will interlock with the previous strip.

Conclusion: The chains will be hung around the classroom.

Goldilocks slept.	The Three Bears left their house.	Goldilocks walked into the three bears' house.
The bears came home.	Goldilocks sat on Papa Bear's chair and broke it.	Goldilocks tried Mama Bear's bed but didn't like it.
Goldilocks ate all of Baby Bear's Porridge.	Goldilocks tried Baby Bear's bed.	Baby Bear cried when he saw his chair was broken.
Goldilocks ran out of the house.	The bears found Goldilocks in Baby Bear's bed.	Papa Bear's porridge was too hot.

Figure 6.1.   Sequence Worksheet

GRADE LEVELS K–3: LESSON FOUR

Multiple Intelligences: bodily/kinesthetic, mathematical/logical, interpersonal, verbal/linguistic

Objectives: Students will be introduced to webbing. Students will create a "body web."

Procedure: The teacher begins by introducing the concept of webbing on the board. The teacher draws an oval in the center and creates lines reaching outward from within the oval. She/he explains that the main idea is put inside the oval and that one detail about the main idea is placed on each line. The teacher reviews the story of "Little Red Riding Hood." After the story is completed, the teacher puts the words "Little Red Riding Hood" in the oval. She/he asks the students to describe what kind of person Little Red Riding Hood was, and she places each characteristic on a separate line—kind, loving, friendly, and so forth. After this is finished, the teacher will ask for volunteers and someone will hold the words "Little Red Riding Hood" and stand in the center of the room. Another volunteer will hold the word "friendly" and stand a few feet away from "Little Red Riding Hood." Continue this way until all words are held. Little Red Riding Hood also holds a number of pieces of yarn or string, and as each individual word is placed, the volunteer picks up the other end of the yarn, so a visual web is created.

Conclusion: Students and the teacher discuss when webs are helpful.

GRADE LEVELS K–3: LESSON FIVE

Multiple Intelligences: bodily/kinesthetic, interpersonal, intrapersonal, verbal/linguistic, musical/rhythmic

Objectives: Students will create a web. Students will work cooperatively in groups. Students will learn the "Webbing Song."

Procedure: Students will be divided into cooperative learning groups. Each group will be given one of the five sets of cards listed below. Each group creates a "body web" using the cards. The group will have to decide which card belongs in the oval and which cards are "lines." Each group is also given yarn, so a visual web is created.

Set 1: rectangle, square, circle, triangle, shapes, oval
Set 2: purple, yellow, green, orange, blue, colors
Set 3: lion, bear, tiger, cat, animals, dog
Set 4: daisy, rose, flowers, lilac, carnation, sweet pea
Set 5: apple, orange, fruit, banana, grapes, cherries

Conclusion: Each student will be given a sheet of paper to draw one of the webs.

"Webbing Song" (to the tune of "Frere Jacques"):

> Organizing
> Organizing
> Classifying
> Classifying
> Helps me see the patterns
> Helps me see the patterns
> Helps me think
> Helps me think

GRADE LEVELS K–3: LESSON SIX

Multiple Intelligences: visual/spatial, intrapersonal, mathematical/logical

Objectives: Students will order information on a "pizza graphic." Students will check individual student understanding of organizers.

Procedure: Each student will be given a copy of the "pizza graphic" (see figure 6.2). Students will need to place words on the correct section of the "pizza graphic." On either the board or an overhead, list the following words or names: Snow White, Cinderella, characters, wolf, Peter Pan, and Hansel. Tell students they are to put one word/name in each section. Remind them that they are creating a graphic organizer.

Conclusion: After papers have been collected, ask the students to share the answers they wrote.

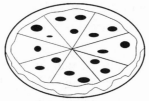

Figure 6.2.   Pizza Graphic

GRADE LEVELS K–3: LESSON SEVEN

Multiple Intelligences: visual/spatial, interpersonal, mathematical/logical

Objectives: Students will create a graphic organizer using comic strip characters. Students will work cooperatively in groups.

Procedure: Students may choose any graphic organizer form or create one of their own. Students will cut out a minimum of six characters from the comics. Students are to create a graphic organizer using the characters.

Conclusion: Students will share their organizers with their classmates.

GRADE LEVELS K–3: LESSON EIGHT

Multiple Intelligences: verbal/linguistic, visual/spatial, intrapersonal, mathematical/logical

Objectives: Students will classify items in the classroom and outside the classroom. Students will create a graphic organizer for the items.

Procedure: The teacher will give each student a sheet of typing paper. Students will follow the teacher's directions as she/he demonstrates how to fold the paper. First, students will fold the paper in half hamburger style (see figure 6.3). Next, the students will fold the paper in half again. Then, students will open the paper so that it is folded in half. The students will take a scissors and cut on the fold line in the middle. This creates two front flaps with a whole back. On one of the front

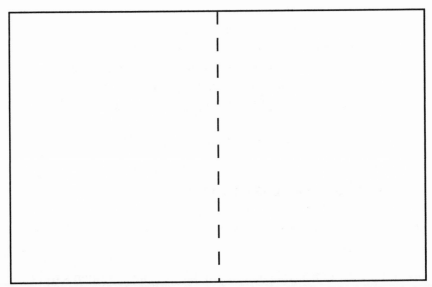

Figure 6.3.   Hamburger Style

flaps, students will write objects inside the classroom; on the other front flap, students will write objects outside the classroom. Students may either draw the objects or write their names.

Conclusion: Pair students up and have each one share his/her graphic organizer. Talk about what objects students have in common and what objects are different.

GRADE LEVELS K–3: LESSON NINE

Multiple Intelligences: visual/spatial, interpersonal, verbal/linguistic, mathematical/logical

Objectives: Students will learn to classify information. Students will create graphic organizers. The teacher will assess students' abilities to create and use graphic organizers correctly.

Procedure: Each group will be given one of the sets of words below. Together, students are to design a brand new, never-used graphic organizer that depicts the information.

Set 1: lakes, seas, ponds, bodies of water, oceans, rivers
Set 2: trees, oaks, elms, maples, dogwoods, pines
Set 3: table, chair, desk, bed, couch, furniture
Set 4: puppies, kittens, cubs, young animals, calves, lambs
Set 5: socks, shirts, pants, sweater, clothes, coats
Set 6: necklaces, rings, pins, earrings, jewelry, bracelets

Conclusion: Each group will share its graphic organizer.

GRADE LEVELS K–3: LESSON TEN

Multiple Intelligences: visual/spatial, verbal/linguistic, mathematical/logical

Objectives: Students will create a graphic organizer. Students will classify hair color.

Procedure: The teacher will begin by asking the students to help her/him create a graphic organizer of everyone's hair color in the class. What is the first step in this process? Hopefully, students will suggest that they must first sort everyone by hair color. What is the next step? Students may decide to make a graph, or they may decide to make a web. The teacher proceeds with either idea. Students give the teacher directions for creating the graphic organizer.

Conclusion: Students and teacher discuss how easy it is to organize information in this way.

GRADE LEVELS 4–6: LESSON ONE

Multiple Intelligences: visual/spatial, interpersonal, intrapersonal, verbal/linguistic

Objective: Students will create an information map using inductive thinking.

Procedure: The teacher begins with the following story: "I want to tell you about a toy shop owner. Mr. Miller is thirty-eight years old. His son,

Charles, is entering first grade. Tell me everything you know about Mr. Miller and his family." After the students are allowed to think for a few minutes, they are divided into think–pair–share groups. Each group lists as many ideas as possible about Mr. Miller and his family. After ten to fifteen minutes, the teacher pulls the students back into a large group. Students give answers as the teacher writes their responses on an overhead. Once all the information has been put on the overhead, students are divided into groups of four and create a visual graphic with the information.

Conclusion: Students share maps with the rest of the class.

GRADE LEVELS 4–6: LESSON TWO

Multiple Intelligences: verbal/linguistic, interpersonal, intrapersonal, mathematical/logical

Objectives: Students will make predictions about automobile accidents. Students will create a graphic organizer using the information from the newspapers.

Procedure: The teacher will divide students into four groups. Once in the groups, students will create hypotheses using the following questions:

1. At what time do most accidents happen?
2. What percentage of accidents involves drunken driving?
3. Do more male drivers or female drivers have accidents?
4. What percentage of accidents involve death?
5. What percentage of accidents happen in the fall, winter, spring, or summer?

After the students have made their predictions, give each group thirty daily newspapers from the same month. The months should represent each of the seasons. Group members will read about accidents and record the necessary information to answer the above questions. After recording the information, students should make a visual graphic of the information. What does the information tell us about accidents in your area? Does the information allow you to create a new hypothesis? If so, what is it?

Conclusion: Write a new hypothesis on the board. Next week, look at newspapers to determine whether or not the hypothesis is valid.

GRADE LEVELS 4–6: LESSON THREE

Multiple Intelligences: visual/spatial, verbal/linguistic, interpersonal, mathematical/logical

Objective: Students will create a stock-and-flow diagram.

Procedure: Instruct the students as follows: "Today, students, we are going to discuss stock-and-flow diagrams, and then each group will create one. This diagram is meant to help see the big picture. Every system has inflows and outflows. The inflows and outflows are similar to cause and effect. In looking at a system that is growing, one wants to determine what is accumulating and what is causing the increase. Or if a system is disintegrating, what is causing the decrease? Let's do a stock-and-flow diagram together. Over the past three years, enrollment has increased in our district. Let's look at what might be causing that to happen. Ideas might include people moving in, a greater birth rate five years ago, or a company moving into the town." Draw a stock-and-flow chart on the board using student responses. A sample diagram appears on page 109 (see figure 6.4). Divide students into four or five groups. Give each group one of the following ideas and have them create a stock-and-flow chart.

1. The town's population is decreasing.
2. Smaller stores are closing.
3. The district is building a new school.
4. There is a shortage of nurses.

Conclusion: Each group shares its stock-and-flow chart with the entire class.

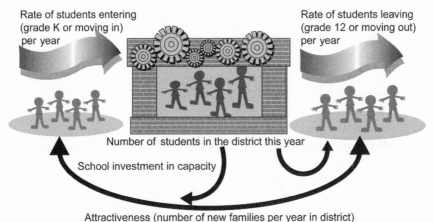

Figure 6.4. Stock-and-Flow Diagram

GRADE LEVELS 4–6: LESSON FOUR

Multiple Intelligences: visual/spatial, interpersonal, mathematical/logical

Objectives: Students will create a graphic organizer using comic strip characters. Students will work cooperatively in groups.

Procedure: Students may choose any graphic organizer form or create one of their own. Students will cut out a minimum of six characters from the comics. Students are to create a graphic organizer using the characters.

Conclusion: Students will share their organizers with their classmates.

GRADE LEVELS 4–6: LESSON FIVE

Multiple Intelligences: visual/spatial, verbal/linguistic, mathematical/logical intrapersonal

Objective: Students will create a "pizza" organizer about each important character in a novel.

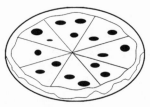

Figure 6.5. Pizza Graphic

Procedure: Students are to list the main characters in the novel they are reading. Students will create a pizza organizer (see figure 6.5) for each character. Encourage students to make the organizers attractive. Give students suggestions as to the type of information that should be included in the organizer. Display the organizers.

Conclusion: Have students discuss the advantages of using organizers to track important information.

GRADE LEVELS 4–6: LESSON SIX

Multiple Intelligences: visual/spatial, interpersonal, intrapersonal, verbal/linguistic

Objectives: Students will use visual/graphic organizers to organize information. Students will classify items in appropriate categories.

Procedure: Students will be placed in small groups to create visual or graphic organizers for a list of words they will receive. All groups will work with the same list of words. Words should be nouns taken from the various academic areas of study. Some examples are multiplication, addition, experiment, microscope, globe, ocean, country, story, poem, drawing, song, game, verb, noun, and character.

Once the students are given the list, they are to work together in their small groups to find a way to visually organize the list. They may use any graphic organizer they feel is appropriate. All words in the list must be placed within the visual organizer.

Conclusion: Each group will present its visual organizer to the whole class along with its rationale for choices.

GRADE LEVELS 4–6: LESSON SEVEN

Multiple Intelligences: visual/spatial, verbal/linguistic, interpersonal, intrapersonal

Objectives: Students will create a graphic organizer depicting the plot of a novel/story they are reading.

Procedure: Instruct the class as follows: "Today we are going to use the novel we are reading to try to help someone who has not read it to understand what happens in the story. You will be asked to work with another person to create this graphic organizer. You should first discuss the story in as much detail as you can to determine as much of the plot as possible. You may want to make an outline of this information. Once you have made as complete an outline as you can, you must find a way to visually represent this plot (your outline)." Creativity and accuracy should be stressed here. Students may need help from the teacher, and the whole class, to start this process before moving into pairs to work.

Conclusion: Student pairs will hang their graphic organizers in the room, and the class will take a tour of the organizers.

GRADE LEVELS 4–6: LESSON EIGHT

Multiple Intelligences: visual/spatial, interpersonal, intrapersonal, verbal/linguistic

Objectives: Students will compare/contrast two events in history. Students will visually represent the information found on events in history.

Procedure: Students will be placed into groups of four and given two events in history per group. They will be instructed to research these events in their texts for information that could be classified as similarities and differences. Each group will then create a visual organizer to represent the information it has found concerning the events.

Conclusion: Groups will share their visual organizers with the whole class, explaining the organizers and the information they discovered.

GRADE LEVELS 4–6: LESSON NINE

Multiple Intelligences: visual/spatial, interpersonal, intrapersonal, bodily/kinesthetic, verbal/linguistic

Objectives: Students will visually represent directions of a game. Students will create a visual organizer for the steps necessary to play a game.

Procedure: Instruct the class as follows: "Today, we are going to spend a little time thinking about what we like to do in our spare time. Many of us like to play games when we have free time. Today, we are going to use the visual/graphic organizers we have been working with to represent our favorite games."

Ask students to find at least one other person to work with. Choices should be made based upon the games students like to play. Once the groups have been chosen, students should spend time discussing the rules of the game and what it looks like when they play it. They may want to make a list or outline of this information.

Finally, students should take the information they have and create a visual organizer to do the following:

- Explain the rules of the game for someone who cannot read.
- Detail what the game looks like for someone who cannot read.

Conclusion: Students will share their visual organizer with the class. Members of the class will give feedback on the clarity and accuracy of the visual organizer for each game.

GRADE LEVELS 4–6: LESSON TEN

Multiple Intelligences: visual/spatial, verbal/linguistic, interpersonal, intrapersonal

Objective: Students will create causal loop diagrams from the story they are reading.

Procedure: Instruct the class as follows: "Today we are going to look at the story we have been reading. We have discussed in the past the definition of "cause and effect," but let's review. "Cause and effect" refers to when one event causes something else to happen." Review with the class some examples from stories it has read or from events studied in history/social studies.

Once you are sure the class knows what cause and effect is, continue with the concept that there are times when what appears to be the effect has another role: the cause for another event. Use the visual graphic for the causal loop here (see figure 6.6).

Place the graphic organizer on the overhead and have the students fill it in as a class with you, making sure that you explain carefully that each step along the loop works backward and forward. Use an example you were given at the beginning of class, or use another you have chosen from social studies, recent news, or your stories.

Finally, take the story that the class is currently learning and discuss together what happens in the story. Then break the students into pairs, each of which is to design a causal loop diagram for this story. Remember, there may be more than one possible diagram, depending upon the number of "cause and effect" episodes in the story.

Conclusion: Students will share with the class their diagrams and the rationales for their choices.

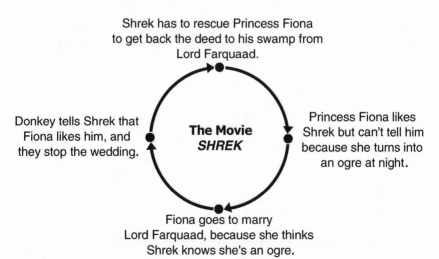

Figure 6.6.   Causal Loop Diagram for the Movie *Shrek*

GRADE LEVELS 7–12: LESSON ONE

Multiple Intelligences: verbal/linguistic, visual/spatial, interpersonal, intrapersonal

Objectives: The students will learn what a behavior over time graph (BOTG) is and how it is used. The students will create a BOTG as a class for a given passage.

Procedure: The teacher starts the lesson with a large group discussion of the use of graphs: when and why are they used? How are they created? What kinds are the students familiar with? The teacher points out that graphs are not used only in science and math. Some examples of graphs from social studies might be population growth in a country, changes in industry in a nation over time, and the distribution of money spent by the state government. In the area of reading, some examples of graphs include how much each character in the story contributes to the conflict and/or the resolution, changes that take place in the antagonist during the story, and trends in character behavior that affect the outcome of the story.

The teacher introduces the BOTG (see figure 6.7), explaining the purpose and uses for such a tool: to help visualize the trends for a given topic so that when decisions have to be made, information is available to help predict the outcome of the decision.

The students are given a brief passage to read and asked as a class to create a BOTG concerning the passage. The teacher puts the students' suggestions either on an overhead transparency or on the board.

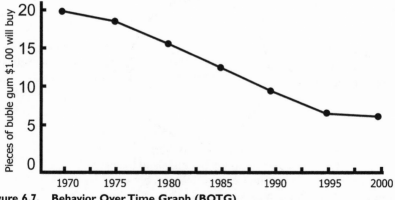

Figure 6.7.   Behavior Over Time Graph (BOTG)

Conclusion: The teacher facilitates a discussion with the students about what kind of information would be included in a BOTG and why it is useful. Finally, the teacher reminds the students of the purpose of the BOTG.

GRADE LEVELS 7–12: LESSON TWO

Multiple Intelligences: verbal/linguistic, intrapersonal, interpersonal, visual/spatial

Objectives: The students will read a short story and create a BOTG for the antagonists in the story. The students will use the BOTG and the information from the story to discuss the conflict and its resolution.

Procedure: Explain to the students that they are going to read a short story today that has a focus on a conflict. As they read, they are to put their focus on the antagonists (major characters in conflict), making notes as needed.

When students are finished reading the story, each one should create a BOTG for the antagonists, tracing their behavior throughout the story. Make sure that the students pay particular attention to the conflict and its resolution. Students might want to put these parts in another color or highlight them.

Conclusion: When students have completed the BOTG, facilitate a discussion with the whole class focusing on what individuals included in their BOTGs and why. Make sure to convey to the class that there are no right or wrong BOTGs, unless students did not complete theirs or used incorrect information.

GRADE LEVELS 7–12: LESSON THREE

Multiple Intelligences: verbal/linguistic, intrapersonal, interpersonal, visual/spatial

Objective: Students will learn what a causal loop diagram is and how it is used.

Procedure: Introduce a causal loop diagram (see figure 6.8) by facilitating a discussion with the students about cause and effect. Make sure to include details about the influence of an effect as another possible cause. Include examples such as:

- The Iraqi War
- SARS
- The search for terrorists
- Inflation
- Lowering the legal alcohol limit to 0.08
- Raising the age for a driver's license to eighteen

Give the students a scenario including a cause and effect, and create as a class a causal loop diagram on the overhead or board. Be sure that the

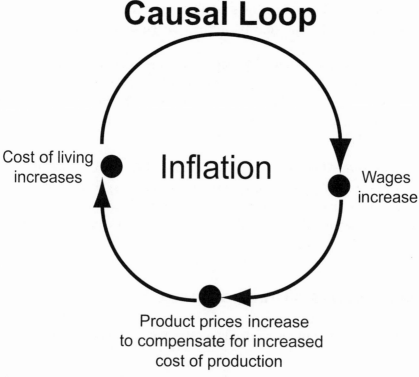

Figure 6.8.   Example of a Causal Loop Diagram

loop has all the necessary elements and that you point out to the students that this loop means that one element can be a cause and effect at the same time. It is best to work your way around the created loop at least two times so the students get this connection.

Conclusion: Have each student share with his/her partner an incident in his/her personal life that has a cause and effect, to see if the incident can be put into a causal loop diagram. Have some pairs share with the whole class.

GRADE LEVELS 7–12: LESSON FOUR

Multiple Intelligences: interpersonal, verbal/linguistic, visual/spatial

Objective: Students will work with partners to create a causal loop diagram from a newspaper article.

Procedure: Explain to students that causal loop diagrams can be made for many circumstances. Refer to some articles you have already found in the newspaper or magazines such as *Time* or *Newsweek*. Examples might be:

- "Target: Saddam," *Newsweek,* April 14, 2003, pp. 51–57.
- "Whose Flag Is Bigger?" *Newsweek*, April 14, 2003, p. 71.
- "Will SARS Strike Here?" *Newsweek*, April 14, 2003, pp. 72–75.

Students will be placed in pairs and given a newspaper article to read. Once the pair has read the article, they are to create a causal loop diagram.

Student pairs will then choose at least one other pair to share their diagram with, explaining what elements they included and why. In addition, each pair should explain to the other how each element fits into the causal loop diagram.

Conclusion: Place causal loop diagrams on a bulletin board in the room so that students can look at them during any free time. Encourage questions from students at the end of the session.

GRADE LEVELS 7–12: LESSON FIVE

Multiple Intelligences: visual/spatial, verbal/linguistic, interpersonal, intrapersonal

Objectives: Students will use knowledge of and skill with causal loop diagrams to create a diagram for a historic event. Students will recognize how causal loop diagrams can help in resolving conflict by allowing them to look at elements of an event in more than one way.

Procedure: This lesson could take two to three days, depending upon how long it takes student pairs to do their research. Students will be placed in pairs. The teacher will assign each pair of students an event from history that involves a conflict. Students will be required to research the details of the event and make sure that the major elements are included in this research. Elements should include cause(s), who was involved, the conflict, how the event unfolded over time, and steps taken to resolve the conflict. Students may use the Internet, textbooks, or any other reference materials for such research.

Once the research has been completed, student pairs are called upon to create a causal loop diagram for this event. Encourage students to be as detailed as necessary.

Conclusion: Student pairs will present causal loop diagrams to the class. Diagrams can be posted on a bulletin board when presentations are complete.

GRADE LEVELS 7–12: LESSON SIX

Multiple Intelligences: interpersonal, intrapersonal, visual/spatial, verbal/linguistic

Objectives: Students will learn what a stock-and-flow diagram is and why we use it.

Procedure: Introduce the stock-and-flow diagram concept through "input–output." Give the students the following example: if you put information into a computer, what do you get out? If you put money into a business, what do you get out? If you put time into a project or venture, what do you get out? Ask the following questions:

1. How do we get an increase?
2. How do we get a decrease?

Show the students a stock-and-flow diagram (see figure 6.9).

Walk through an example of the diagram and its elements as well as why we use it. An example of a stock-and-flow diagram would be: a family in your town has had a tragedy and is in need of a fundraising effort. One of the children in the family is in your class. The class decides that if it pulls together and puts in the effort and time, it will get results for the fundraising needed. A committee is formed and decides to run a car wash for the weekend, both Saturday and Sunday, from 9 a.m. to 6 p.m. Each car will be washed for a donation of $3.00. The car wash will take place in the school parking lot, so lots of student volunteers can help.

Conclusion: Ask students to provide examples of when a stock-and-flow diagram would be beneficial.

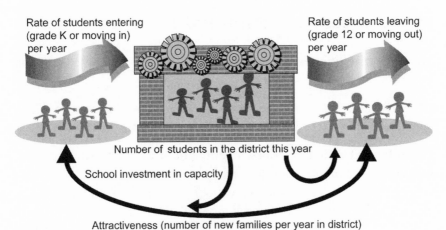

Figure 6.9.   Stock-and-Flow Diagram

GRADE LEVELS 7–12: LESSON SEVEN

Multiple Intelligences: visual/spatial, interpersonal, intrapersonal, verbal/linguistic

Objectives: Students will create a stock-and-flow diagram from a story. Students will share/explain their diagrams with other students in small groups.

Procedure: Remind students of the example given in class the previous day of a stock-and-flow diagram. Hand out to students a story for them to read. Once the students have read the story, they are to create a stock-and-flow diagram.

Once the students are finished with their diagrams, they can form their own groups of three to four students to share what they each came up with. Each student in the group is responsible for explaining his/her own diagram and how it works. Focus should not be on whether any one diagram is the correct one, but that all necessary information is included in each diagram.

Conclusion: Students will be asked to volunteer to share stock-and-flow diagrams. Remind them that there is no *right* diagram, and that all that matters is whether the necessary elements are included.

GRADE LEVELS 7–12: LESSON EIGHT

Multiple Intelligences: verbal/linguistic, intrapersonal, interpersonal, bodily/kinesthetic, visual/spatial

Objective: Students will work in cooperative learning groups to determine the patterns/trends/history of an event given by the teacher.

Procedure: The teacher does a review of visual tools—maps, webs, flow charts—to prepare the class for the outcome desired for this lesson. Remind students that, as with an iceberg, we must look underneath the surface to find out what the problem might entail.

The teacher divides the class into groups of three students and allows each student in the group to choose a role: history, patterns, or trends. Explain that the assignment they will be given will require them to work separately on their own parts, but collaboratively in the end to present their information both orally and visually. Groups will also be required to orally summarize their visual tool. This lesson could take one to three days, depending upon events chosen and research required.

The teacher chooses events from the local school district, the local city/town, or the state. These are then handed out to groups of three students. Research materials should be provided by the teacher so that students may research the event assigned to the group to determine history, patterns, and trends.

Conclusion: Students will present the map/web/flow chart to the class.

GRADE LEVELS 7–12: LESSON NINE

Multiple Intelligence: intrapersonal

Objective: Students will learn what double-loop reflection is and how to use it.

Procedure: The teacher introduces this lesson as a final piece to the section on systems thinking. This process involves a person or group reflecting/thinking about the assumptions they have made when making a decision, the conclusions they have drawn after gathering information, and the reasoning they have used to come to a plan of action.

Using an overhead, the teacher should present the graphic for this strategy. This visual will serve as a reference point for the introduction of the three-step process involved in the double-loop reflection strategy (see figure 6.10).

The first step that should be introduced is reconsidering. This might involve the student/group answering these questions:

Is our approach to this project appropriate?
Why do we feel it is the right way to do this project?

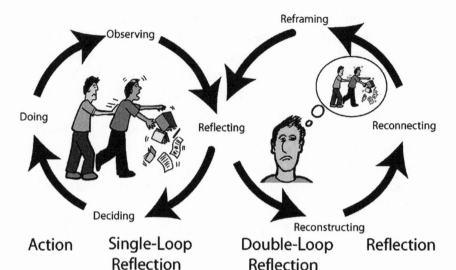

Action   Single-Loop   Double-Loop   Reflection
            Reflection   Reflection

Figure 6.10. The Three-Step Process Involved in the Double-Loop Reflection Strategy

What is the reality that underlies our choices?
What will be the consequences of a new approach?
What will be the costs of making this change, and is it worth the cost?

The second step is reconnecting. Students look at their project and approach to it to see if there might be another way to approach it. Some possible questions to address are:

Who else has tried something such as this using a different approach?
How does that approach differ from ours?
How did they implement their approach?
Are there signals or trends that we should be noticing?

The final step is reframing. Here students will be asked to look at expanding their current ideas. The following questions would be addressed:

How else might we approach our project?
Is it the right project, the right goals, and the right objectives?

What role do we want to play in a new situation for this organization? What conditions keep us from learning?

Conclusion: Once these three steps have been explained, the teacher should walk through them using an example. A possible topic that the class could practice with might be a current school policy that the students would like to change. A specific example might be the policy for open campus during lunch periods.

7

CASE STUDIES FOR ELEMENTARY AND SECONDARY SCHOOL TEACHERS

USING CASE STUDIES

It is important that the teacher be very familiar with the case material before using it with the class. Once the teacher has a good grasp of the case, he or she must decide what key concepts are to be brought out in the discussion. It is advisable to create an outline, with the key concepts listed in order of importance so that, if those concepts at the bottom of the outline do not fit into the discussion time frame, the most important concepts will be discussed.

The teacher will facilitate the discussion about the case. This means the teacher must be prepared to ask questions of the students. Questions should prompt student thinking in the direction of the key concepts identified in the outline the teacher has created. Remember, a good discussion will not follow a set pattern such as the outline. The outline should drive facilitation and questioning as needed. Use of a board or overhead will help the students stay focused on the flow of the discussion for the case. As the students contribute their thoughts and their answers to questions posed, the teacher should write facts and ideas that will help students further the discussion.

Seats in the classroom are arranged in a U shape for case study discussion. The idea is that everyone can see each other during the discussion. This promotes active participation and interaction. Early on in the year, it might be practical to have name tents on the tables/desks in front of the students so that everyone can address each other by name.

The teacher must decide before the case discussion how students will contribute. Will the teacher ask for volunteers or call on students so all will participate? If the class is large, it is likely that some students will not volunteer. The teacher can facilitate active participation of all students by asking specific students questions if they have not volunteered. Of course, the teacher should be aware of student body language and students' abilities in this kind of discussion.

CHAPTER 2 (PERSONAL MASTERY): ELEMENTARY CASE STUDY

Paul is in Mr. Taggart's fifth-grade class. The school year has started, and the students have begun the hard work required of them in both their science and social studies classes. During these two classes, Mr. Taggart's students are allowed to work in groups to get their work done. Mr. Taggart started out the year choosing the members for groups, but after two months has allowed the students to choose their own groups.

Paul has had some difficulty with this part of the work in both science and social studies. He has always chosen his friends to work with, and the work gets done, but something has been happening lately that is bothering the others. An example of what happens to Paul is the following exchange:

Paul: I choose for Steve, Manny, and Fred to be in my group. I want to get an A, and they are the ones who will help me get it.

Manny: I don't want to be in your group, Paul. You rely on everyone else to get your work done for you, so you can get the grade you want.

Steve and Fred: We are tired of trying to carry you when you don't do your share. You work some of the time we are in a group, but we always have to pick up the slack.

Paul: But I need to get good grades to get into a good college, and I know you are my friends and are willing to help me. If I don't do well, my parents are going to kill me!

Steve: We are your friends, but this is fifth grade and if you are thinking about going to college, you need to think about what you need to do to achieve your own goals.

CHAPTER 2 (PERSONAL MASTERY): SECONDARY CASE STUDY

Sarah is a ninth grader at Miner High School. As an eighth grader, Sarah experienced some difficulties with getting passing grades, especially in English. She had difficulty keeping up with the reading assignments each night and understanding some of what she read. She is hoping that this year will go more smoothly as she enters high school. She has been thinking about what she wants to do once she leaves high school. Her parents want her to go to college like her brother does. They keep telling her that there will be no jobs without college, but she isn't so sure about going to college because she struggles with school. She has asked her friends about their plans for the future, but no one seems to really have a plan. She has also spoken to the ninth-grade guidance counselor. He wasn't any help, as she came out of that visit more confused than when she went in.

Sarah likes to work with children and small animals and is talented in the area of art. She loves to draw and paint. She has spent some time in middle school in the classes that would allow her to explore this talent. But now she is in high school and faces the challenge of choosing classes that will get her somewhere. The question is where. She has registered for her classes for ninth grade and is happy with her choices: English 9, Algebra 1, Earth Science, American History, PE, and Drawing. She has one study hall.

Sarah has just begun to think about what she wants and who she wants to be. She feels lost and confused. She doesn't know what to do from here.

CHAPTER 3 (MENTAL MODELS):
ELEMENTARY CASE STUDY

Miranda arrived at school on the first day of fourth grade worried she would have no luck making friends. Her family had moved to Sumner over the summer. This would be her third school in five years of school (K–4). She gets ready for the first day and walks to school.

As Miranda enters the school, many students turn to look at her with strange faces. She has seen these looks before—Who is this kid? Where did she come from? One girl with long dark hair smiles at her and says hi. Miranda's first thought is, "She must be one of the unpopular kids, she said hi to me." She keeps walking without really acknowledging the girl.

The first bell rings, and Miranda shows at the class of Ms. Stanton's, her fourth-grade teacher. Ms. Stanton smiles and walks her to a seat in the second row. Oh, it is right in front of that girl with the long hair who said hi. Her first thought is, "If I become friendly with someone who isn't popular, I haven't got a chance."

CHAPTER 3 (MENTAL MODELS):
SECONDARY CASE STUDY

As an eleventh grader, Mick is asked by Mr. Adams, the PE teacher, to help in a ninth-grade PE class that has forty students. Mick agrees, and then asks Mr. Adams what his responsibilities will be. Mr. Adams explains that Mick will be responsible for working with half of the class and completing the same work as Mr. Adams will complete with the other half.

On the first day of class, Mr. Adams decides that the two groups will go to the football field to do calisthenics. As Mick gets his half of the class ready in rows, he realizes that Brian is in this class. Brian is a ninth grader who Mick has had run-ins with in the neighborhood in the past. Brian is a bigger guy than many his age and has used that to his advantage. Mick has watched Brian bully others and has tried help when he could.

Mick walks by Brian and gives his most intimidating look, while Brian looks confused. As the group begins jumping jacks, Mick walks by Brian again. Brian is somewhat annoyed and asks, "What?" Mick keeps on walking.

CHAPTER 4 (SHARED VISION): ELEMENTARY CASE STUDY

Stan Roha is a fifth-grade teacher at Palmer Elementary School. He has been working with his class this year on respect and teamwork. He began the school year with them by giving a complete explanation of his goals and his expectations for a successful year for the class. In the first days of school, Mr. Roha tried to get his class to help him make class rules and expectations, but there was a lot of arguing and unruly behavior during the process. So Mr. Roha took control and did this on his own, without student input.

In Mr. Roha's fifth-grade class, students are expected to complete some of their work independently and some cooperatively. This means that students are to work together as needed, and yet when independent work is called for, they are to create an environment conducive to productivity.

After nine weeks, Mr. Roha's students are still taking more than five minutes to settle down to work after an assignment has been given. Additionally, when placed in cooperative learning groups to complete an assignment, students complain and finish an average of only 50 percent of the work in each session. Each student in the class seems solely interested in his/her own learning.

CHAPTER 4 (SHARED VISION):
SECONDARY CASE STUDY

Mrs. Elliot's third block English class has been troublesome since the very first day. Mrs. Elliot had hoped her students, as tenth graders, would come with a sense of community and work well with each other, especially in small groups. This hasn't been the case. Many of her students in this class, when asked, preferred to work alone. Some students, at least half, are not internally motivated to be in school and do their best. During the first few days of class this term, Mrs. Elliot tried to have class discussions about her expectations and theirs, as well as the environment necessary for success in the class. She had to stop this plan after she looked up during the second day to a sea of faces with the eyes rolling and less than thrilled looks on their faces.

English 10 is structured in such a way that students complete work in class in either small groups or a large group discussion. Students are expected to read all assignments outside of class and come to class prepared to participate fully for the benefit of all members of the class. To date, students have failed to comply with the small group work at least two days per week. When large group discussions have been scheduled, a handful of students have done the discussing, due to an apparent lack of caring and preparation on the part of the rest of the class.

CHAPTER 5 (TEAM BUILDING):
ELEMENTARY CASE STUDY

Mrs. Anderson is a third-grade teacher at Lawson Elementary School. She is interested in helping her students learn to work together as part of a team. Since the first day of school this year, many of her students have had trouble getting along with each other. When given the option of choosing a person to work with to complete an assignment or working alone, most choose to work alone. Difficulties have also arisen on the playground, at PE, and in music class. There have not been fights, but students have expressed negative attitudes about sharing, cooperating, and being together as a group.

Mrs. Anderson has had a meeting with the whole class to discuss why people should learn to work in teams. She gave many examples and even had the students contribute their own. Once this meeting was over, she asked the students to pair up to work on a project. The students seemed very reluctant. Determined to help her students take the first step, Mrs. Anderson had the students number off in ones and twos. The ones lined up along one side of the room and the twos lined up along the other. She then instructed all twos to take three giant steps forward and stop. She gave the same direction to the ones. The students were then face to face with a partner.

Students were asked to sit next to the person they were facing so they could work together. There was a lot of moaning and complaining. When Mrs. Anderson gave the instructions for the project and assigned each partner a role, students did not begin their work.

CHAPTER 5 (TEAM BUILDING): SECONDARY CASE STUDY

Mr. Rand is a history teacher at Port Washington High School. He understands the value of building teams with his students as they prepare to enter life beyond high school. His plan is to incorporate this team building in his daily lessons with his students.

Mr. Rand's second period tenth-grade history class is full, with twenty-eight students in the room. Most of these students he would describe as "chatty." Trying to get them to focus when he lectures is difficult enough, but it is even more difficult when trying to get them to produce something when they are working in cooperative groups. He has assigned members to each group and then assigned roles to each member. This seems to help each time the groups start the work, but eventually the groups break into old habits, and they start talking about other things, such as their personal lives.

Mr. Rand has spoken to this class about his expectations and the reasons for having them work in teams. Some students seem interested when he is speaking about team building, its purpose, and the end product. But they don't, as a class, appear to be motivated to follow through when assigned the work.

CHAPTER 6 (SYSTEMS THINKING):
ELEMENTARY CASE STUDY

Mrs. Vincent has a fourth grade class at Hoover Elementary School. One of this year's goals for her class is for her students to understand and use a "whole picture" approach to solving problems. She has found in the past that her students often begin the blaming game and don't often get to the heart of a problem or even come to understand how the problem arose in the first place. She starts the year with a class discussion about her expectations for her students and facilitates a further discussion in which the students contribute their own expectations. As she begins the second day of school, Mrs. Vincent begins working with her students on teamwork and building a sense of community. She places students in groups of four to complete an assignment for her science class. Students are very productive during this time period. She is happy with the results.

After the first week of school, Mr. Smith comes to Mrs. Vincent to speak to her about her class. Mr. Smith is the music teacher. He has come to see her because he was very concerned about the inappropriate amount of talking and giggling her students were doing during his music class. Mrs. Vincent listened carefully to Mr. Smith and suggested that he work up a consequence list for the class. This seemed like a good idea to Mr. Smith.

The first day of the second week of school, Mr. Smith spoke with Mrs. Vincent's class during music. He told them about the behavior he was unhappy with and showed them his consequence chart. He explained that with each infraction of the rules there would be an increase in the severity of punishment. He asked the students if there were any questions. There were none. As class started, the usual behaviors began to occur. Mr. Smith began to implement his plan, giving out the first consequence. The class groaned, but quieted down. This was the only incident on this day. Over the next week, there were a few incidents of inappropriate behavior in music class and, as promised, the consequences increased.

The next week of school, the students in Mrs. Vincent's class thought Mr. Smith would forget about his plan, so they began with their behavior the first day. They were amazed that he gave them the next punishment on the list! They went back to Mrs. Vincent's class grumbling and angry. When Mrs. Vincent asked what was wrong, the students told her that Mr. Smith was being unfair. He didn't have the right to treat them the way he was. They went on and on about the consequences, never mentioning their inappropriate behavior.

CHAPTER 6 (SYSTEMS THINKING): SECONDARY CASE STUDY

Mrs. Benjamin teaches speech class for seniors at Johnson High School. She emphasizes to her classes that their speeches should take into account the audience for whom they are being prepared. She lets the students know that this is an important part of their grade. Students who fail to take their audience into consideration can lose a whole grade for their final grade.

One speech during the semester is to persuade the audience about a certain topic using one's own point of view and some research. There is also an opportunity to have an authentic audience, such as the principal, if the students wish to change some policy or rule. Students don't lose any points for this speech if they choose to just use the class as their audience.

Tim is a senior in Mrs. Benjamin's class. He has been bothered that the seniors are not allowed off campus during lunch. He decides to do his speech on this topic, hoping he will change some minds about the current practice. He prepares his speech, thinking about the students in his class and why they want this privilege. He is very excited about the speech and tells Mrs. Benjamin he would like her to invite the principal so Tim will have a chance to change his mind.

The day for Tim's speech arrives, and he goes to the front of the room. The principal is sitting in the back of the class, eagerly awaiting the research and persuasion Tim will use in his speech. Tim starts with a list of the reasons why the seniors would like to leave campus during lunch. He then moves on to why it is unfair that they don't get to leave. He finally speaks about the rights the seniors should have because they are seniors and have earned them.

After his speech is finished, he asks the principal if his speech and the information in it have changed the principal's mind about seniors leaving campus over lunch. The principal says they have not and leaves the class, thanking Tim for inviting him. Tim is very angry and cannot understand the reaction from the principal. After all, he invited him to listen and put in a lot of good reasons why the seniors wanted this. Mrs. Vincent reminds Tim about the research they were supposed to do for every speech. She tells Tim that there were reasons for not having open campus and that Tim didn't address any of these in his speech. In fact, there was a history of behavior that Tim should have addressed to make his point.

ANNOTATED BIBLIOGRAPHY

DREAMS (CHAPTER 2)

Ben-Ezer, Ehud. *Hosni the Dreamer: An Arabian Tale.* New York: Farrar, Straus, and Giroux/HarperCollins, 1997.
Hosni finally realizes his dream of traveling to the city, where he spends his gold dinar in a way that changes his life forever.

Bradby, Marie. *More than Anything Else.* New York: Orchard, 1995.
Booker T. Washington (1956–15) dreams of the day he'll be able to read.

Dr. Seuss. *Yertle the Turtle.* New York: Random House, 1958.
Peace is accomplished by maintaining self-control.

Hickam, Homer H. *Rocket Boys: A Memoir.* New York: Delacorte, 1998.
A young boy dreams of building rockets. This book became a movie called *October Sky.*

Khalsa, Dayal Kaur. *Cowboy Dreams.* New York: Crown Books for Young Readers, 1990.
A little girl wants to grow up to be a cowboy.

Levine, Arthur. *Mrs. Moscowitz's Last Stand.* New York: Tambourine, 1993.
Mrs. Moscowitz believes she can make a difference in her neighborhood. She sets out to save a tree the city wants to destroy.

Mitchel, Margaree King. *Uncle Jed's Barbershop.* New York: Scholastic, 1993.
Uncle Jed pursues his dream of saving enough money to open his own barbershop.

Striegel, Jana. *Homeroom Exercise.* New York: Holiday, 2002.
Regan must face the possibility of never achieving her dream of becoming a professional dancer.

Wojciechowska, Maia. *Shadow of a Bull.* New York: Simon and Schuster Children's Books, 1964.
Manolo must decide whether to follow in his father's footsteps and become a bullfighter or to follow his heart and become a doctor.

Yee, Paul. *Ghost Train.* Toronto: Groundwood, 1996.
Fourteen-year-old Choon-yi saves her father's spirit after a railroad accident in North America.

Young, Karen Romano. *Beetle and Me: A Love Story.* New York: Morrow 1999.
Fifteen-year-old Daisy pursues her goal of single-handedly restoring the car of her dreams, the old purple Volkswagen Beetle from her childhood.

LADDER OF INFERENCE (CHAPTER 3)

Baker, Betty. *The Pig War.* New York: HarperCollins Children's Books, 1969.
Living on an island together are the American farmers and the British traders. War begins when the American farmers shoot a British pig.

Blaine, Margaret. *The Terrible Thing That Happened at My House.* New York: Scholastic, 1975.
This is a story of what happens to a family when they are too busy to listen to each other.

DePaola, Tomie. *The Knight and the Dragon.* New York: Putnam Juvenile, 1980.
A knight and a dragon decide to have a fight. Each one prepares carefully for the fight. In the end, with some help, they figure out how to make peace.

Dr. Seuss. *The Butter Battle.* New York: Random House, 1984.
Two nations dispute how buttered bread should be eaten, and they keep building bigger weapons.

Dr. Seuss. "The Zax." In *The Sneetches and Other Stories.* New York: Random House, 1961.
Two Zaxes going the opposite directions run into each other. Neither one will move an inch to the left or to the right. Both are stuck.

Jones, Rebecca. *Matthew and Tilly.* New York: Dutton's Children's Books, 1991.
Matthew and Tilly are good friends. Sometimes they get into disagreements that in the end strengthen their friendship.

Lionni, Leo. *Six Crows.* New York: Knopf, 1988.
Six crows and a farmer have a disagreement over a field of wheat. A wise owl helps them find a solution.

Wildsmith, Brian. *The Owl and the Woodpecker.* New York: Scholastic Library, 1971.
Owl moves into a new home. He doesn't realize that woodpecker will peck away during the day while Owl wants to sleep. Unfortunately, other animals become involved in Owl and Woodpecker's conflict.

UNDERSTANDING OTHERS' PERSPECTIVES (CHAPTER 3)

Ginsburg, Mirra. *The Chinese Mirror.* New York: Harcourt, 1988.
A Korean folktale tells about a mirror that reflects a different point of view to everyone who looks in it.

Guback, Georgia. *Luka's Quilt.* New York: HarperCollins Children's Books, 1994.
Luka and her grandmother learn to appreciate each other's perspectives and value each other's vision.

Van Allsburg, Chris. *Two Bad Ants*. Boston: Houghton Mifflin, 1988.
This story presents a fascinating depiction of the ants' view of the world as they explore it together.

Zolotow, Charlotte. *The Hating Book*. New York: Sagebrush Education, 1969.
Two girls have a misunderstanding. Finally, one of the girls asks the other one why she is being so mean. The misunderstanding is cleared away.

SHARED VISION (CHAPTER 4)

Bunting, Eve. *Smokey Night*. New York: Harcourt, 1994.
People who feel hostility toward each other are brought together through a common misfortune.

Dr. Seuss. *And to Think That I Saw It on Mulberry Street*. New York: Random House, 1937.
Children must envision a goal before they can achieve it.

Pinkwater, Manus. *The Big Orange Splot.* New York: Scholastic, 1977.
In this neighborhood, all of the houses look alike. Suddenly, a person paints his home to reflect himself. The neighbors are upset with the person's vision.

COOPERATION (CHAPTER 5)

Bennett, Cherie. *Zink.* New York: Random House, 2001.
Sixth grader Becky faces her battle with leukemia with the help of a trio of zebras from the Serengeti.

Brown, Marcia. *Stone Soup.* New York: Simon and Schuster, 1947.
Three hungry soldiers come to a town where all the food has been hidden, and they set out to make soup of water and stones. Before long, the whole town is involved, and together they create delicious soup.

du Bois, William Pene. *Bear Circus.* New York: Penguin Putnam Books for Young Readers, 1971.
After the grasshoppers eat everything and the kangaroos save the koalas from starvation, the bears put on a circus to show their appreciation.

Ginsburg, Mirra. *Across the Stream.* New York: Green Willow, 1982.
This is a story of chickens and ducks helping each other.

Henkes, Kevin. *Sheila Rae's Peppermint Stick.* New York: HarperCollins, 2001.
Two sisters argue over candy until they find a way to be a part of an ogbo, or age grouping.

Johnson, Ryerson. *Monkey and the Wild, Wild Wind.* London: Abelard–Schuman, 1961.
During a storm, a group of animals seek a cave for protection. They disagree, and they dislike each other because of their differences. A playful monkey unites them and helps them work as a team.

Konigsburg, E. L. *The View from Saturday.* New York: Simon and Schuster Children's Books, 1996.
Four students represent their sixth-grade class in the Academic Bowl competition.

Medearis, Angela. *Seven Spools of Thread: A Kwanzaa Story.* Morton Grove, Ill.: Whitman, 2000.
The seven Ashanti brothers put aside their differences, learn to get along, and embody the principles of Kwanza when they are given the seemingly impossible task of turning thread into gold.

Quattlebaum, Mary. *Jackson Jones and the Puddle of Thorns.* New York: Random House Children's Books, 1999.
Jackson Jones hopes to earn enough money to buy a basketball by growing a garden; however, all he seems to get is trouble.

Rohmann, Eric. *My Friend Rabbit.* Brookfield, Conn.: Millbrook, 2002.
Being a good friend, Mouse shares his plane with rabbit. Unfortunately, the plane lands in a tree. The whole neighborhood tries to help get the plane out of the tree.

Scribe, Murdo. *Murdo's Story: A Legend from Northern Manitoba.* Winnipeg, Manitoba: Pemmican, 1985.
Once upon a time, the animals lived in two lands. In one of the lands, it was always summer, and in the other land, it was always winter. Of course, the animals in the winter wonderland want to steal the bag that contains summer.

Slepian, Jan. *The Alfred Summer.* New York: Simon and Schuster Children's Books, 1980.
Lessons in courage and perseverance are learned as four adolescents unite to build a boat together.

Woodson, Jacqueline. *Lena.* 2nd ed. New York: Random House, 2000.
Thirteen-year-old Lena and her younger sister, Dion, mourn the death of their mother while running away from their abusive father.

Young, Ed. *Seven Blind Mice.* New York: Philomel, 1992.
> This story retells the Indian fable of the blind men discovering different parts of an elephant. The men argue about what it is they are touching because each man sees it differently.

SYSTEMS THINKING (CHAPTER 6)

King-Smith, Dick. *Three Terrible Trins.* New York: Crown Books for Young Readers, 1994.
> Three mice brothers ignore the class system and befriend a lower-class mouse. Together, they form a team to fight cats.

Stanley, Jerry. *Hurry Freedom: African Americans in Gold Rush California.* New York: Crown Books for Young Readers, 2000.
Mifflin Gibbs arrives in San Francisco in 1950 and works toward achieving equality in the court system.

REFERENCES

Senge, P. 1990. *The Fifth Discipline.* New York: Doubleday.

Senge, P., N. Cambruon-McCabe, T. Lucas, B. Smith, J. Dutton, and A. Kleiner. 2000. *Schools That Learn: A Fifth Discipline Fieldbook for Educators, Parents, and Everyone Who Cares about Education.* New York: Doubleday.

Siccone, F., and L. Lopez. 2000. *Educating the Heart.* Boston: Allyn & Bacon.

ABOUT THE AUTHORS

Ellen M. O'Keefe is working on her doctoral dissertation at the University of Iowa in Iowa City. She is a member of the College of Education Faculty at Mount Mercy College in Cedar Rapids, Iowa. She grew up in Newburyport, Massachusetts, where she also began her special education teaching career in grades K–4. Her educational career includes teaching special education in grades K–12 over twenty years. O'-Keefe received her master's degree in learning disabilities from the University of Northern Colorado in 1979. Her interests include teaching, reading, needlepoint, and cooking.

Mary Catherine Stewart, O.P., is a member of the College of Education faculty at Mount Mercy College in Cedar Rapids, Iowa. She grew up on a farm in Nokomis, Illinois, and entered the Dominican Sisters of Springfield, Illinois, in 1975. Her educational career includes teaching in both elementary and secondary schools and serving in administration in elementary schools. Stewart received her doctorate in curriculum and instruction from the University of Sarasota. Her interests include teaching, reading mysteries, and baking.